Hegel's Theory of Normativity

Hegel's Theory of Normativity

The Systematic Foundations of the Philosophical Science of Right

✦

Kevin Thompson

NORTHWESTERN UNIVERSITY PRESS
EVANSTON, ILLINOIS

Northwestern University Press
www.nupress.northwestern.edu

Printed in the United States of America

10 9 8 7 6 5 4 3 2 1

Library of Congress Cataloging-in-Publication Data

Names: Thompson, Kevin (Kevin Brian), author.
Title: Hegel's theory of normativity : the systematic foundations of the philosophical science of right / Kevin Thompson.
Description: Evanston, Illinois : Northwestern University Press, 2019. | Includes bibliographical references and index.
Identifiers: LCCN 2018056003| ISBN 9780810139923 (paper text : alk. paper) | ISBN 9780810139930 (cloth text : alk. paper) | ISBN 9780810139947 (e-book)
Subjects: LCSH: Hegel, Georg Wilhelm Friedrich, 1770–1831. Grundlinien der Philosophie des Rechts. | Law—Philosophy. | Natural law. | Normativity (Ethics)
Classification: LCC K230.H43 T46 2019 | DDC 340.112—dc23
LC record available at https://lccn.loc.gov/2018056003

For Virginia Nell (Hankins) Thompson

1928–2015

CONTENTS

ACKNOWLEDGMENTS

The following study is part of a longer project devoted to Hegel's theory of political sovereignty. It is the product of many years of labor. During this time, I have had the privilege of developing the ideas in it through conversations with a large number of colleagues and students and at several institutions.

The departments of philosophy at the University of Memphis, where this project first began, Washington University in St. Louis, Southern Illinois University, and, finally, DePaul University have all supported this work in various ways. I am immensely grateful to each of them for the opportunities they afforded me and the collegiality they all displayed; each of these departments was a rich and distinctive intellectual community in which to develop this project.

Among the many colleagues that I have had the privilege of working with over the years, I want to thank Pauline Kleingeld, Peg Birmingham, Rick Lee, Pat Werhane, and Will McNeill for their unwavering support. Two organizations have been immensely helpful to me in my work on this project: The Hegel Society of America, and especially Stephen Houlgate, Robert Williams, Angelica Nuzzo, Ken Westphal, but, above all, Ardis Collins, and the Chicago Area Consortium in German Philosophy, and its founder and director, Rachel Zuckert. Thank you to Mark Alznauer for his encouragement and for really making the publication of this book possible and thanks also to Trevor Perri and Anne Gendler of Northwestern University Press for their graceful shepherding of this project and their unfailing advice. And I want to especially thank Michael Naas for the suggestion that made this work possible, and Robert Bernasconi, who nurtured and continually challenged my ardent devotion to the study of Hegel's thought, and in the process taught me everything about what it means to be a truly critical scholar.

I am immensely grateful for all the students in the Hegel seminars that I have led at Washington University in St. Louis and at DePaul University for their questions, their comments, and their challenges to this work. The project advanced immeasurably due to their vigorous contributions. I especially want to thank Sina Kramer, Andrew LaZella, Nathan Ross, Kieran Aarons, Floyd Wright, Tom Krell, Dilek Huseyinzadegan, Miguel Gualdrón, Owen Glyn-Williams, Jacob Singer, Ryan Froese, and Ashley Fleshman.

Finally, the most difficult acknowledgments. Difficult only because I cannot begin to measure the immense debt that I owe to my family for their patience, their support, their humor, and their love. This book is for them: my wife, Regina, and our children, Ethan and Emma. And, lastly, it is for the one who taught me what it means to love, to commit, to persevere: my father, James R. Thompson.

An earlier version of chapter 1 appeared as "Systematicity and Normative Justification: The Method of Hegel's *Elements of the Philosophy of Right*," in *Hegel's Political Philosophy: On the Normative Significance of Method and System*, ed. Thom A. Brooks and Sebastian Stein (Oxford: Oxford University Press, 2017), 44–66. I am grateful to the editors and to Oxford University Press for permission to publish a revised version of that essay here.

ABBREVIATIONS

All references to Hegel's works are included in the text according to the following scheme of abbreviation. Citations are to the appropriate paragraph, indicated by the § sign, to the appropriate Remark (*Anmerkung*), indicated by "A," and, where necessary, to the appropriate page number. Note that although I have consulted standard English translations, all translations from these texts are my own.

Enz. 1817 *Enzyklopädie der philosophischen Wissenschaften im Grundrisse (1817)*, ed. Wolfgang Bonsiepen and Klaus Grotsch, *GW*, vol. 13.

GPR *Grundlinien der Philosophie des Rechts*, ed. Klaus Grotsch and Elisabeth Weisser-Lohmann, *GW*, vol. 14:1.

GW *Gesammelte Werke*, ed. Deutsche Forschungsgemeinschaft in collaboration with the Nordrhein-Westfälischen (earlier Rheinisch-Westfälischen, 1968–95) Akademie der Wissenschaften (Hamburg: Felix Meiner, 1968–).

Hegel's Theory of Normativity

Introduction

✦

Hegel and the Problem of Normativity

The aim of this work is to set out the basics of Hegel's theory of normativity. To do so, I offer an interpretation and defense of the systematic foundations of what Hegel called the "philosophical science of right," that is, his moral, legal, social, and political philosophy. By "systematic foundations" I mean the doctrines and procedures upon which the science of right rests and that, in turn, make it possible, but which this science does not itself explain. The present study sets forth an exposition and examination of the three most important of these foundations: the science of right's method of justification and the categories that govern its specific claims and theories; namely, the concepts of freedom and right. In doing so, this study strives to remain faithful to the core critical intention and intellectual context of Hegel's broader philosophical project. Its central thesis is that Hegel's innovative conceptions of normative argumentation, practical agency, and social ontology[1] provide the keys to understanding and evaluating his theory of normativity and his science of right as a whole. The remainder of this book is devoted to developing this insight and to demonstrating both its textual fidelity and philosophical viability.

Yet perhaps no other aspect of Hegel's science of right has been more controversial than the relationship between its substantive normative claims and the metaphysical doctrines of his philosophical system.[2] Accordingly, as an initial step in this project, I shall begin by briefly laying out the problem of normativity and reviewing the current major interpretive approaches to Hegel's science of right as a response to this issue. I will then introduce the distinction between representation and systematicity that not only distinguishes these approaches, but will figure as pivotal to the accounts of Hegel's method of normative justification, freedom, and right that form the core of the present study. I follow this with an outline of the basic argument of the book and conclude with a brief discussion of the sources upon which the study is based.

The Problem of Normativity and the Status of the Science of Right

It is obvious that our lives are suffused with normativity. We exist amidst a wealth of practices and institutions, all of which make claims upon us. That is, they purport to possess authority to place us under obligation to comply with their requirements in our conduct and even in our very character. To be more specific, normativity is the feature of institutions, principles, practices, and states of affairs that provides us with reasons to comply with what they command. It is their binding force that entitles them to specify our moral, legal, and political duties. But from whence does this authority arise? What is the justification of this power? This is the problem of normativity or, more precisely, the problem of the source of normativity, and it is the question to which Hegel's theory of right seeks to respond.[3] Because right (*Recht*), for Hegel, is nothing other than the concept which denotes that certain principles, practices, institutions, and states of affairs possess valid binding authority over us.

Hegel is quite clear that the foundations of his account of normativity lie in the systematic structure and metaphysical doctrines of his general system of philosophical sciences. Accordingly, he tells us that the science of right is to be judged solely in terms of its "philosophical manner of progressing from one matter to another and of conducting a scientific proof, the speculative way of knowing in general" (*GW* 14:1, 5). But rather than including an exposition of this method in the *Elements of the Philosophy of Right* itself, he notoriously takes a "familiarity with scientific method" (*GW* 14:1, 6) for granted: "As for what constitutes the scientific procedure of philosophy, that is presupposed here on the basis of philosophical logic" (*GPR* §2A). As a result, the exact nature and status of the discipline's core claims were left ill-defined, and a legacy of interpretive disputes, which can all be traced back to the earliest reviews of the work, has been its consequence.[4]

The terrain of the current literature reflects this troubled history. Studies of Hegel's political philosophy can be divided today into four main tendencies defined by two distinct axes: systematic vs. nonsystematic, and metaphysical vs. nonmetaphysical. The first tendency—the *metaphysical-systematic*—holds that the systematic order of Hegel's thought is essentially tied to the metaphysical claims that it makes about the nature of reality, and together these provide the foundation for his political theory.[5] Its central contention is that, without the systematic framework and the more rudimentary claims about what is actual that comprise the philosophical sciences of logic, nature, and spirit, the authoritativeness of the doctrines of the science of right stands vacuous and unwarranted. The second tendency—the *systematic-nonmetaphysical*—agrees that the systematic structure of Hegel's work is significant for its normative claims, but believes that this can be detached from its metaphysical core.[6] It treats the apparently metaphysical doctrines of the philosophical sciences as categories by which moderns must interpret and manipulate their environment, and it holds that the epistemic necessity of the concepts at issue in the science of right is sufficient to establish them as normatively binding. The third tendency—the *nonsystematic-metaphysical*—attributes little significance to the systematic form of Hegel's work, holding, instead, that its real import lies in its core metaphysical commitments.[7] It interprets these concepts and doctrines most often in a broadly Aristotelian vein and then employs them to explain the principles and claims of Hegel's political philosophy. Finally, though it acknowledges Hegel's systematic and metaphysical ambitions, the fourth tendency—the *nonsystematic-nonmetaphysical*—finds both endeavors to be dismal failures and, instead, seeks to extract what it claims to be the philosophically valuable and coherent insights from the rubble.[8] It then reconstructs these kernels via some form of conceptual analysis, phenomenological description, or social scientific explanation in order to attempt to establish their contemporary viability.

The present study develops an interpretation that takes the systematic character of Hegel's thought and the metaphysical commitments that issue from it to be absolutely essential not only to understanding the core claims of his philosophical science of right but, more importantly, to assessing their philosophical merits. Without the justificatory support of the broader system of which it is but a part, Hegel's moral, legal, social, and political philosophy becomes nothing more than a compendium of assertions, a collection of interesting and perhaps even insightful theses, that nonetheless lack any of the grounding necessary to establish their veracity or normativity. Furthermore, without its systematic mode of argumentation and the metaphysics that follow from this, the resultant interpretation presents a significantly distorted account of the science's central concept: right loses the binding authority accorded it by its being the objective embodiment of freedom and becomes an arbitrary constraint on human conduct. My contention is that understanding the link between systematic structure, normative justification, practical agency, and social ontology stands as the litmus test for any reading that hopes to do justice to Hegel's thought. More specifically, it is the only way that we can hope to fulfill the twofold ambition of a genuinely philosophical history of Hegel's science of right: to remain faithful to the intention and context of the figure, texts, and tradition(s) under examination, and at the same time, allow the thought being interpreted, despite the general non-metaphysical tenor of much contemporary work in social and political philosophy, to speak with its full force beyond its own historical context. It is for these reasons, then, that the present study stands clearly in the wake of the systematic-metaphysical tendency, and the proof of its merits will lie in the historical and philosophical cogency of the interpretation that it proposes.[9]

Let me note, however, that the interpretation that I will develop has, nonetheless, been enriched by the three other tendencies in varying ways. What it rejects is the way in which each of these tendencies ultimately leaves the authoritativeness of Hegel's science of right exposed to skepticism's classical justificatory challenges. The reason for this is that the other three tendencies are all what Hegel would call "representationalist" interpretive paradigms, and their result is that they undermine the normative status of right itself.

Now, to see what this claim means, we need to introduce a distinction that is central to Hegel's general philosophical project and that will serve as the basis for the interpretation of the science of right that will be developed in the present study: the distinction between representational and systematic forms of knowledge (*Enz. 1817,* §§1–3).

Hegel uses the concept of representation (*Vorstellung*) in two distinct ways, one broad, the other narrow. In the narrow sense, representation refers to an organism's cognitive power, set over against sensible intuition and pure thought, to depict or refer to objects or states of affairs via images, symbols, signs, or words, and, in its most complex form, through narration (*Enz. 1817,* §§373–83). In the broader sense, representation denotes any form of knowledge that takes the validity and soundness of its method of inquiry or its object of investigation for granted, rather than in need of demonstration. These two senses are, of course, related, but our primary concern here will be with the broader sense.

Systematic forms of knowledge, for Hegel, are arrangements of concepts, propositions, and doctrines where the justification of each element of the system not only follows from its place within the systematic whole, as a long philosophical tradition has held,[10] but where the validity and soundness of the whole itself derives from its being presuppositionless.[11] That is, systematic forms of knowledge are genuine or scientific forms of knowledge because they are dedicated to engaging in fully self-critical thinking, and this requires setting aside and disengaging from all inherited conceptions, all ways of taking up a position with respect to ourselves and to the world. The radicality of Hegel's philosophical enterprise flows, then—as Hegel himself so often reminded us—not primarily from the principles, concepts, or even the doctrines that it propounds, but from its commitment to a distinctive method, "the only true one, the one identical to its contents" (*Enz. 1817,* 5), as he put it, one that presupposes absolutely nothing, what he called "the resolve *to will to think purely*" (*Enz. 1817,* §36A).

Hegel contends that representational forms of knowledge necessarily render themselves vulnerable to classical skeptical attack and, as a result, philosophy must necessarily be systematic (*Enz. 1817,* §7A). For any justification offered on behalf of a knowledge claim, whether the claim is normative, epistemic, metaphysical, or of some other kind, the skeptic undertakes to show that this grounding is either an unwarranted assertion (that the grounding is arbitrary, merely a *hypothesis*), or a foundation that itself stands in need of justification (that the grounding opens onto an *infinite regress*), or that it is an account that presupposes the very thing that it seeks to establish (that the grounding is actually viciously *circular*). Hegel's claim is that representational forms of knowledge make themselves necessarily vulnerable to this challenge—what has been termed the "Agrippan trilemma"—precisely insofar as they assume their subject matter or their mode of demonstration or both.[12] Systematic forms, in the distinctive sense of systematicity that will be developed in what follows, foreclose this possibility through their commitment to take absolutely nothing for granted. The distinction between the representational and the systematic is thus, at its core, primarily epistemic, and it has certainly been, as such, contestable that any kind of presuppositionless stance is tenable, let alone philosophically cogent. But for now, the basic point for Hegel is rather simple: systematic forms of knowledge are secure against skeptical attack, while representational forms are not.

With this basic outline of the distinction now in place, we can return to the question about the contemporary models for interpreting Hegel's philosophical science of right: in what sense can the systematic-nonmetaphysical, the nonsystematic-metaphysical, and the nonsystematic-nonmetaphysical tendencies be said to be rooted in any kind of representationalist forms of knowledge and thus open to skeptical challenge?

Simply put, despite the profound differences between them, these interpretive models all take for granted a preconception of the world that they then seek to employ in explicating Hegel's thought. More precisely, they assume a common world of experience—a fund of intuitions, customs, and traditions, a life-world, to borrow a term—in relationship to which they seek to interpret and assess Hegel's thought. The nonsystematic-metaphysical and the nonsystematic-nonmetaphysical tendencies obviously both discount the significance and even the viability of the systematic dimension of Hegel's project. But this is precisely what leads them to be uncritical hermeneutical approaches, for in abandoning the systematic in their account of Hegel's thought, they also abandon its commitment to presuppositionlessness in their exposition.

The nonsystematic-metaphysical tendency, for instance, tries to show that Hegel's social and political concepts and doctrines provide explanatory frameworks that better capture the social and political features of the contemporary life-world than other rival interpretive paradigms. The paradigm case that has often been advanced by purveyors of this view has been the idea that Hegel's account of the rational state offers the best articulation of the bonds that rightly hold together modern political communities.

The nonsystematic-nonmetaphysical tendency makes use of selected features of this common world as touchstones for reconstructing Hegel's social and political insights, whether via social science or phenomenology, seeking thereby to render them more amenable to contemporary standards. Accordingly, its adherents have taken the sense and value of various concepts—for example, self-actualization, reconciliation, and freedom—as basic and have sought to show how Hegel's political philosophy can be built out from these foundations.

Yet in pursuing these avenues, both of these tendencies take the very normativity of the life-world itself for granted and, as such, they expose their interpretations to the skeptic's trilemma: that this world is either a wholly arbitrary hypothesis, a ground that itself stands in need of justification, or simply that it assumes the very conclusion that stands in need of proof. In abandoning its systematic character, then, they sacrifice the very feature of Hegel's work that grants it its claim to be genuinely authoritative and not just a sheer compendium of probabilistic assertions. And, most importantly for our present concerns, in forgoing the systematic foundations of Hegel's work, these approaches also render the concept of right itself as nothing more than an unwarranted constraint on freedom, rather than its immanent ground.

Now, it would seem that the systematic-nonmetaphysical approach spares itself this fate because it clearly endorses the centrality of systematicity to Hegel's enterprise. Yet, it too remains a representationalist approach. It holds that the systematic relations of Hegel's political philosophy are not sufficient to grant it standing as normatively binding. Rather, Hegel's claims gain this status, according to this view, by being what has come to count historically as the conditions necessary to make the self-understanding of distinctly modern communities—namely, that its members recognize one another as free agents—valid. Which is to say that the systematic-nonmetaphysical approach, in the end, is a broadly historicized transcendentalist stance: it interprets Hegel's science of right as accepting a given—here the practices and shared recognitive practices of a concrete historical community—that then seeks after its conditions of possibility. But, of course, in taking this self-conception for granted, the systematic-nonmetaphysical tendency exposes its reading, just as do those outlined above, to the skeptic's trilemma and thereby also sacrifices the ultimate foundations of right itself.

The systematic-metaphysical approach that we shall be pursuing here sees clearly that normativity, for Hegel, requires not only the secure epistemology afforded by systematicity, but also the ontological moorings that follow directly from it. It thus rejects the historicized transcendental stance of the systematic-nonmetaphysical tendency, as well as the dogmatic metaphysics of the nonsystematic-metaphysical approach. And it holds, perhaps paradoxically, that it is only by remaining faithful to the core ambitions of Hegel's philosophical project—that is, to a properly critical metaphysics—that the cogency and value of his claims for us now about freedom, institutions, and a genuinely rational social order can be properly assessed. Since the remainder of the present study will serve as a defense of this thesis, it will be useful to outline its basic argument.

An Outline of the Argument

The study that follows seeks to demonstrate the essential relationship between Hegel's accounts of normative justification, practical agency, and social ontology and to show how these philosophical foundations provide the keys to understanding and evaluating his science of right as a whole.

This book's first chapter, "Method," provides an interpretation and defense of the distinctive form of argumentation that Hegel employs to justify normative claims. It compares standard forms of normative justification to Hegel's systematic conception. By situating Hegel's work within the lineage of post-Kantian political philosophy, the epistemic and ontological commitments of this method are identified, and from these an account of its unique way of establishing norms is developed. The basic argument is that justifying a normative claim, for Hegel, requires showing that it necessarily arises from and is thus set within an interrelated set of concepts, a system of knowledge, that fulfills the criteria that reason demands for a justification to be fully satisfactory.

The next two chapters show how this method of systematic justification is used by Hegel to work out the relationship between freedom and authority and to explore the distinctly metaphysical underpinnings of this relationship. Chapter 2, "Freedom," examines the basic elements of Hegel's theory of freedom. Central to Hegel's account is the concept of individuality. Individuality, Hegel contends, is the ontological structure that captures the distinctive activity of autonomous action, and to make sense of this concept requires unpacking Hegel's broader theory of practical agency, specifically his account of moral psychology and his treatment of the problem of reflection and its proper measure. This, in turn, will lead us to what is clearly the central issue of Hegel's science of right, the account of the objectivity or actuality of freedom, the deduction of the concept of right, the order that Hegel calls Objective Spirit.

The task of chapter 3, "Right," is to develop an account of the link between understanding right as the foundation of freedom and the thesis that this entails that right be objective, in the sense of being both universally valid and actually existent. The chapter is thus an examination of what Hegel calls Objective Spirit, and it explores the standing, nature, and structure of this systematic and uniquely ontological concept as it establishes the fundamental framework for Hegel's political philosophy proper and his theory of political authority in particular.

This book's "Conclusion" shows how this systematic account of the foundations of right can in turn function as a type of critical theory. That is to say, it shows how the philosophical science of right is able to serve as the basis for making normative judgments about the practices and institutions of actual social and political orders. To do this, I propose a distinction between a systematic and a public use of reason, and I argue that Hegel's thought lays down distinctly systematic foundations for the justification of the public employment of reason to sustain the principles of rationality that have historically come to shape the world in which it operates, and to propose specific reforms of that heritage which seek to make good on the promises borne within it.

A Note on Sources

Before we begin, a word is in order regarding the textual sources upon which the present study draws in order to make its case. This is necessary both because this study differs from what has become common practice and because it restricts its usage of the available materials.

The present study's account of the philosophical foundations of Hegel's science of right seeks to set out and explain these doctrines as they were articulated in the *Elements of the Philosophy of Right* (1821) and the first edition of the *Encyclopedia of the Philosophical Sciences in Outline* (1817). I have selected these texts because I believe that, philologically, they form a coherent and clear unit of thought and are the most reliable statements of Hegel's mature moral, legal, social, and political philosophy. To understand the significance and limitations of this approach, a brief survey of the available textual resources is necessary.

Scholars of Hegel's mature social and political philosophy currently have three main categories of texts at their disposal:

(1) Published writings: These include the sections on Subjective and Objective Spirit from the *Encyclopedia of the Philosophical Sciences in Outline*, in its three editions (1817, 1827, and 1830), the *Elements of the Philosophy of Right*, which is officially listed as published in 1821, as well as various reviews, introductions, and the essays entitled "Proceedings of the Estates Assembly in the Kingdom of Wurttemberg, 1815–1816" (1817) and "On the English Reform Bill," which was published (under censorship) in 1831.

Both the *Encyclopedia* and the *Philosophy of Right* are comprised of paragraphs to which Hegel appended what he called *Anmerkungen* (Remarks), which are mainly explanatory in nature.

(2) Handwritten notes, drafts, and fragments: These include what have come to be called Hegel's lecture notes, a draft of a response to a review of the *Philosophy of Right*, and a few fragments.

When the *Philosophy of Right* was published in 1820, Hegel arranged to have a personal copy produced that was divided into two volumes, both interleaved with blank pages. On the interleaved pages he wrote notes for his own use, referring to specific passages on the opposite page, apparently over the course of his lectures. The second volume of this special edition was lost, so only the notes up to §180 (the transition to the account of civil society) remain extant.

(3) Student transcriptions: These are the transcripts made by students of Hegel's oral presentations in the lecture course entitled "Natural Right and Political Science," which he first delivered at the University of Heidelberg in the winter semester of 1817–18, and then continued at the University of Berlin, beginning in the winter semester of 1818–19, and then again for five semesters, the last course being interrupted by his death on November 14, 1830.

It has become commonplace among interpreters of Hegel's political thought to fail to recognize the important philological distinction to be drawn among these materials. Historically, commentators have often treated the excerpts from the student transcripts as equal in stature to the published writings; a few writers have even attempted to appeal to Hegel's lecture notes in this manner. However, in my view, these approaches simply fail to accord proper weight to the qualitative distinction between the published texts that Hegel prepared, the transcriptions by students, and Hegel's own notations.

Philological rigor demands that the student transcriptions be recognized as what they are: possibly imperfect records of oral presentations that were themselves never meant for publication. And while Hegel certainly did indeed treat both the *Encyclopedia* and the *Philosophy of Right* as handbooks to accompany his lectures, this does not authorize us to use this material as authoritative sources for correcting and amending the views articulated in the published works. Rather, this material should be treated as a rich evidential fund for exploring how Hegel's principal social and political doctrines developed over time, as well as providing access to the innovations that he tried out in the classroom. But to do this demands careful reconstruction of the unique trajectories and lines of argument of each course and then the painstaking comparison of these, isolating any transformations and developments that occur.

Hegel's lecture notes, though they are at least in his own hand, are, for the most part, simply too fragmentary to be of use in the interpretation of the theory. I thus believe they should be taken up only after the mature theory of 1820 has been sufficiently clarified, and would even then have to be interpreted in light of the student transcriptions.

What these considerations clearly indicate is that the published texts deserve to be treated as the *exclusively* authoritative sources of Hegel's social and political doctrines. It is they that merit our first and most sustained scrutiny, for it is only to the extent that the published formulations of Hegel's theories and arguments are understood on their own terms that the secondary task of tracing the genesis and development of Hegel's thought in this area can possess a secure gauge for its own pursuits.

Now, from among the published works, I have, as I noted, restricted the present study to the *Elements of the Philosophy of Right* (1821) and the first edition of the *Encyclopedia of the Philosophical Sciences in Outline* (1817) because I believe that their temporal proximity to one another provides us with the best philologically sound and coherent account of Hegel's political theory. The second (1827) and third (1830) editions of the *Encyclopedia* contain extensive expansions and revisions of the accounts provided in the first edition and, as such, represent, in my judgment, significant developments and modifications that merit more careful, concentrated attention than the thematic study undertaken here would permit.

With this review of the available evidence and the way it has been used in constructing the present study, we can now turn to the task at hand.

Chapter 1

✦

Method

The aim of this chapter is to set out the method of normative justification that Hegel employs in his philosophical science of right. By this I mean the form of argumentation by which the validity and soundness of the central doctrines of the *Elements of the Philosophy of Right* are established. But, as we have noted, no other aspect of Hegel's theory of right has been more controversial than the relationship between its core doctrines and what Hegel called its scientific or speculative method or, to put the issue more broadly, the relationship between the substantive normative claims of Hegel's practical philosophy and the metaphysical doctrines of his broader philosophical system.

Accordingly, the task of the present chapter is to consider two fundamental questions: (1) What exactly is speculative method? and (2) How does this method serve as a form of normative justification?[1]

The strategy I will follow in addressing these questions will be to set out a comparison between Hegel's systematic conception of normative justification and the rationalist and empiricist forms of demonstration that have defined the Western tradition of political theory, particularly as these traditions shaped late eighteenth-century and early nineteenth-century German political thought. The chapter's principal thesis is that the distinctiveness of Hegel's methodology lies in the fact that, unlike the traditional approaches, it holds the justification of a normative claim to require showing that it is necessarily entailed as a moment in the immanent unfolding of the concept of freedom within a general systematic order of knowledge. The normative standing of a concept, principle, institution, or practice, for Hegel, on this reading, thus flows from its being established as a necessary moment in an arrangement of knowledge that is itself immune to skeptical challenge precisely by virtue of its systematic form. Normativity, in short, is a product of the systematic structure of the science of right.

The key to this view is Hegel's contention that the traditional forms of normative argumentation fail to establish the authoritativeness of their claims because they are rooted in the dogmatism of representation. As we have seen in the "Introduction," Hegel argues that representation renders any type of authoritative claims vulnerable to the challenges posed by skepticism, and this motivates his commitment to a distinctly presuppositionless form of justification. Accordingly, I begin by setting out an account of normativity and the forms of justification that developed in late eighteenth-century and early nineteenth-century German thought to secure the authoritativeness of fundamental norms and I show why these, on Hegel's analysis, fail. I then use this critique to construct an interpretation of systematicity as a general form of rational justification, and from this I develop, by means of a reading of the opening paragraphs of the *Elements of the Philosophy of Right*, an account of systematicity as a unique form of distinctly normative justification.

Normativity and the Traditional Forms of Justification

The Traditional Forms of Normative Justification: Rationalism and Empiricism

The conceptual space of German political thought in the late eighteenth and early nineteenth centuries was defined primarily by two distinct, yet traditional forms of justification and normativity—rationalism and empiricism—and these provided the foundations for the specific doctrines and movements concerning the nature and purpose of the state and of social order that defined this fertile period. It will be useful to begin, then, with a brief sketch of these traditions.

In what are admittedly broad terms, rationalism, in this context, seeks to derive normative principles from properties it holds to be necessary features of the fundamental order of things, while empiricism claims that such standards derive their standing from various kinds of facts such as sentiment, inclination, tradition, language, or culture. The fundamental difference between these strands can be said to lie in their antithetical conceptions of rationality.[2] For rationalism, reason is principally an intuitive power. It is able not only to engage in discursive thought—such as conceiving, judging, and inferring—but is also capable of perceiving or grasping the fundamental structure of being, the providential order of reality. For empiricism, reason is nothing more than its discursive ability. It simply conceives, judges, and infers things about the data it receives from the senses. Rationalism contemplates the order of things, while empiricism produces order out of random contingency. Each method can thus be said to be rooted in a different form of intuition. For rationalism, it is reason's own intellectual intuition that has insight into the fundamental order of being, while, for empiricism, it is sensible intuition that is the root of reason's creations. These different conceptions in turn lead to different understandings of normativity and correspondingly different forms of justification.

To justify a norm for rationalism is to do nothing less than to see that the principle, concept, institution, or practice making a claim to binding authority is itself specified by or determinable within the providential order of being, the fundamental structure of reality. For instance, the fact that crimes require punishment may be grasped as part and parcel of the objective moral order. But this principle is normative, that is, it is vested with obligatory moral force, because it is itself the ground or it is grounded in the law of nature. Normative justification, on this view, establishes the authoritativeness of something by showing that the claim in question possesses the requisite status within the totality of the moral order of the world or that it is deducible from a claim that does. It follows that, for rationalism, one acts rightly or one's disposition is virtuous when one is in accord with the laws of being discoverable by reason through intellectual intuition.

In the empiricist construal, a principle, concept, institution, or practice is normative to the extent that it is endorsed or is laid down as binding by some individual or corporate willing. Crime requires punishment, on this view, not because some fundamental moral order dictates this, but because an authoritative person or group holds to this principle, concept, institution, or practice as necessary, and required, for instance, for the maintenance of social order. Justification is thus a matter of there being an appropriate desiring of something to be normative and this alone being sufficient to make it so. For empiricism, then, one acts rightly only when one follows conventions; reason here is subservient to the demands of what is found in and through sensible intuition.

Rationalism's insight into the natural moral order was taken, by theorists of Enlightened Absolutism such as Seckendorff, Wolff, Garve, Eberhard, and the cameralists (Justi and Sonnenfels), to support the notion that the authority of the ruler lies in his commitment to providing and promoting the material and spiritual welfare of his citizenry and that these goals were to be achieved through the strict and centralized regulation of industry and trade, price controls, public education, and censorship of the press.[3] State paternalism was thus thought to be the means to secure the principles and attendant blessings of the providential order.

Empiricism, on the other hand, bore a more complex lineage in this period of German political thought since it was the root of both Conservatism and Romanticism. For Conservatives, such as Möser, Rehberg, Gentz, and Wieland, the reliance upon empirical warrant was taken to mean that the authority to rule is properly derived from historical sanction and that the well-being of society was to be ensured by the establishment and support of the ties of tradition afforded by religion, culture, language, and the public rituals whereby a people are bound to one another as a cohesive community.[4] However, for Romantics like Herder, the Schlegels, Schleiermacher, Novalis, Fries, and Savigny, the purpose of the state was to promote and provide for the rights and freedoms of its citizens to form communal associations, and the requisite principles for creating this social order were freedom of the press, religious tolerance, and equality of opportunity.[5] For them, the authority of the sovereign lay in the devotion of the citizenry spurred by the majestic aura that true artists and tradition created around him.

Hegel's decisive insight here was to recognize that these divergent strands of political rationality could all be traced back, in differing ways, to the traditional forms of normative justification. He was thereby able to cut through their ideological and programmatic differences and unearth their underlying fundamental methodological orientations. Following from this, he was able to see that these traditional forms of normative justification took their respective subject matters and procedures for granted because they shared a common reliance upon representation and it was this, he argued, that rendered them all vulnerable to the charges of arbitrariness, regressivity, and vicious circularity, the skeptical trilemma.

Normativity and the Problem of Representation

Hegel's critique of rationalism and empiricism as forms of normative justification can be said to develop in three distinct stages: he first sets out a basic critique of representationalism as a form of philosophical knowledge; from this analysis, he then proposes general criticisms of rationalism and empiricism as distinct kinds of representational knowledge; and then, based on this, he derives specific objections to each as accounts of distinctly normative justification.

In the opening paragraph of the *Encyclopedia of the Philosophical Sciences in Outline* (1817), Hegel draws a sharp distinction between representation and the philosophical forms of knowledge:

> All sciences other than philosophy have objects that are given [*zugegeben*] as immediate from representation [*Vorstellung*], and they are thus presupposed [*vorausgesetzt*] as assumed [*angenommen*] from the *beginning* of science, so that in the course of further development, requisite and needed determinations are taken from representation. (*Enz. 1817,* §1)

The distinction that Hegel wishes to draw in this passage is between bodies of knowledge that are composed of, or at least rooted in representational images and philosophical forms of knowledge, which take concepts rather than representations as their resource and object. A concept, for Hegel, is distinctive in that it comprehends the fundamental essence of a thing without recourse to any kind of symbolic or figurative elements derived from sensible intuition. It is a setting forth of the fundamental structure of a thing purely in terms of its essential properties, where the relationship between these is a matter of logical necessity. By contrast, representational forms of knowledge draw their objects readymade from the power of representation; they thus take over their objects from sensible intuition and thus presuppose, rather than deduce, both the subject matter of their inquiry and the relations between its various objects.

In the Remark to this paragraph, Hegel offers examples of representations as they function as the subject matter or object of inquiry in various sciences: magnitude is taken to be the object of mathematics, space is the object of geometry, number is the object of arithmetic, disease is the object of medicine, animals are the objects of zoology, and plants are the objects of botany (*Enz. 1817*, §1A). He contends that, despite the rather wide array of objects and sciences invoked here, each of these is nothing other than a generic conception that has been forged through generalization and comparison from the raw material of sensible experience. The details of how this works in each case need not concern us here. What is important to note is that all of these objects possess a necessarily indeterminate epistemic, and as we shall see, normative, status. As representations, each of these objects of inquiry stands between the spatiotemporal individuals of empirical intuition and the unbounded universalities of conceptual thought. And this means that these objects are necessarily defined by an admixture of contingent and arbitrary associations, ones either produced in the formative process itself or already present as a feature of the existing empirical source from which they were derived. Hegel's argument is that this intermediate status is what renders not just the objects, but the methods of representational argumentation that draw upon them, impotent before the skeptical trilemma.

Consider first the objects. Representational forms of knowledge take the objects they wish to investigate for granted since representation, as a faculty, continually makes them available; it literally places (*stellen*) them before (*vor*) us for investigation. Accordingly, these objects are always on hand, ready to be explored. But this means that in accepting these objects as they are, their existence is never called into question. They simply are, and, as such, they can be presupposed: "Such a science does not have to justify the necessity of the objects that it treats . . . because they [its objects] are assumed to be existent from representation" (*Enz. 1817*, §1A). But if an account of the very existence of some object is not required, then its warrant to be a valid subject matter for rational explanation is left outstanding and any concepts, inferences, and claims derived from or about this object are necessarily open to the accusation of being mere assumptions rather than genuine knowledge.

If we turn now to the methodologies of such forms of knowledge, we find that the examination of a representational object amounts to nothing more than unpacking the determinations it already contains. With the givenness of the object comes the givenness of its properties. The methodological task, then, is simply to extract these determinations and, by doing so, to claim to have derived genuine knowledge about the subject matter. Hegel provides a succinct description of this process: "At first, such an object is given its *familiar name*. This is fixed, yet it initially gives only the representation of the matter. But more determinations of the matter must be given. These can, certainly, be taken [*aufgenommen*] from the immediate representation" (*Enz. 1817*, §1A). The procedure Hegel describes here is a mix of analysis and observation that, in the end, produces a set of features that can only be contingent generalities, instead of the necessary and essential properties that genuine knowledge requires.

Accordingly, representation renders the method and objects of representational forms of knowledge necessarily arbitrary, unwarranted, and presupposed, which are the core charges of the skeptic. But how does this general critique of representationalism apply to rationalist and empiricist forms of epistemic justification?

Hegel examines the representational underpinnings of rationalism as the rubric common to the metaphysical projects of the classical, medieval, and modern periods. He argues that this form of knowledge takes its object, the structure of reality, from the empirical world by abstracting from it all that it deems to be in conflict with the universality of natural law. This order's existence as well as its intellectual intuitability are thus both taken for granted, and as such, the supposedly natural order of being—defined by its principal objects: the soul, the world, and God—is a foundation lacking a warrant to be what it purports to be. Hegel makes this point quite precisely:

> Its *objects* are certainly totalities, which in and for themselves belong to reason—*soul, world, God*—but metaphysics took them from representation, establishing itself on them as *complete, given* subjects by applying the determinations of the understanding and had only its representation for its criterion as to whether the predicates fitted and were satisfactory or not. (*Enz. 1817*, §20)

Similarly, rationalism's methodology seeks to produce genuine knowledge by taking various properties—such as existence, finitude, simplicity, and so on—all of which have been abstracted from experience, and ascribing them to the natural order, or what Hegel calls trying "to determine the absolute through the attribution of predicates"[6] (*Enz. 1817*, §19). In this sense, rationalism strives to construct an account of the in-itself, the unconditioned, with the finite determinations of representation. It thereby substitutes the contingent for the necessary, the transient for the essential. The result is a rigid, exclusionary conception of truth in which only one side of opposed attributes can be true, a position Hegel designates as the very epitome of dogmatism (*Enz. 1817*, §21).

Empiricism, for Hegel, also takes its object as well as its method from representation, but unlike rationalistic metaphysics, it seeks to preserve the full breadth and density of this sensuous domain through its appeal to the immediacy of experience. Empiricism thus begins as a rejection of the abstractions of rationalism, and searches for a new concrete and sure foundation in sensible, rather than intellectual, intuition. But in doing so, it falls prey to the very same strand of dogmatism because it simply takes the content of perception, feeling, tradition, and sentiment and tries to elevate these contextually bound, particular experiences to the status of universal, eternal principles and concepts, the content of genuine philosophical knowledge. To do this, empiricism has to disentangle the concrete nexus presented by these facets of experience and distill a supposedly essential set of properties. The result is precisely the kind of abstractions that empiricism had sought to reject. Hegel sums up this aspiration and its failure in a rather succinct formulation:

> [Empiricism] takes not only the entire content of representation but also all the content and determination of thought as it is found in

> sensory perception, with feeling and intuition as an external or internal fact of consciousness, or as it believes it can derive it, and it takes these empirical facts in general and their analysis for the source of truth, but either denies the supersensory altogether or at any rate all knowledge of it, and makes only the form of abstraction, identical positing, available for thought. (*Enz. 1817*, §26)

Now, if Hegel is correct in this assessment and the objects and methods of rationalism and empiricism are indeed taken from representation, then they must be either wholly arbitrary, infinitely regressive, or viciously circular. As a consequence, each approach vitiates its own work because the insufficiency of their respective foundations and modes of demonstration must necessarily flow to all the concepts, claims, and inferences that are derivable from them. This means, of course, that not only is the epistemic status of the knowledge that each purports to derive in question, but their normative standing is in jeopardy as well. If the moral order or the empirical world serve as nothing more than covert assumptions or brute assertions, and if rationalist attribution and empiricist analysis amount simply to means for portraying the ephemeral as the eternal, then the authoritativeness of the principles, concepts, and institutions derived from them can make no validly binding claim on the conduct or character of agents.

Hegel draws the implications of this critique of rationalism and empiricism as forms of knowledge for their corresponding concrete species of normative justification in the "Introduction" to the *Elements of the Philosophy of Right*. In the domain of practical philosophy, he contends, rationalist metaphysics, which he calls the "formal" method, takes its principal task to be the formulation of the definition of right itself as opposed to the determination of the rightfulness of specific acts or claims. To define right, in this sense, is thus to grasp it as a principle endemic to the natural moral order. Now, as we shall see, Hegel will agree that the main charge of a genuine science of right is to set out what right itself is, that it must begin from a proper deduction of right. The problem with rationalism as a form of normative justification, for Hegel, is thus not with its aim, but with the way in which it seeks to ground the concept of right. Rationalist normative projects, such as those of Seckendorff, Wolff, Garve, and Eberhard, purport to derive the concept of right by way of intellectual intuition. But this is really nothing more than abstraction and attribution from representation: "But [in this way] the deduction of the definition becomes something reached by etymology, by abstraction from particular cases, so that it is grounded in the feelings and representations of human beings. The correctness of the definition is therefore posited in its agreement with prevailing representations" (*GPR* §2A). As such, right itself is rendered as nothing more than a generic conception and, as such, it is filled with all the contingencies and arbitrariness of the empirical fount from which it is fashioned. Rationalist metaphysics therefore makes of right an unwarranted posit: arbitrary, open to infinite regress, and vicious circularity.

Hegel considers empiricism as a form of normative justification under the guise of two distinct kinds of Romanticism: subjectivism and historicism.[7] Both seek to root the concept of right in sensible intuition because only here, they contend, can it have the kind of concreteness that such principles require in order to move those under their authority to act. As with rationalism, Hegel will affirm the basic intent of this approach: right must be concrete in order to compel action. But subjectivism and historicism seek determinacy in representation; the only difference between them is whether the "source of right" from which its warrant is drawn is personal (subjective) or communal (historical).

Hegel argues that for the subjectivists, like the Schlegels, Novalis, and Fries, the idea of right and its further determinations "are immediately taken up and asserted as *facts of consciousness*, and our natural or intensified feelings, our *own heart* and *enthusiasm*, are made the source of right" (*GPR* §2A), whereas in historicists, such as Herder, Hugo, and Savigny, "the emergence and development of determinations of rights as *they appear in time*," or what Hegel also terms "development from historical grounds," "is confused with development from the concept," a confusion that illegitimately extends "the significance of historical explanation and justification" into "justification which is *valid in and for itself*" (*GPR* §3A). Empiricism, like rationalism, thus constructs right as a problematically determinate figure drawn from the well of representation, rather than as a genuinely rational, grounded concept. And in so doing, empiricism, like the rationalism it seeks to oppose, deprives right of any basis for its claim to possess binding authority over human conduct and character.

Hegel viewed the contested conceptual space of late eighteenth and early nineteenth-century German political theories through the lens of representationalism and found it rife with openings to skepticism. Though Enlightened Absolutism, rooted in rationalist metaphysics, with its "formal definitions, inferences, proofs, and the like," had, he believed, "more or less disappeared" (*GPR* §2A), Conservatism and Romanticism, both tied ultimately to empiricist forms of justification, were, particularly in their subjectivist and historicist forms, ascendant, and their identification of right with personal or communal conviction, he contended, promoted nothing less than a "hatred of law [*Gesetz*]" (*GW* 14:1, 10). He therefore saw the terrain within which he sought to establish the need for his own method of normative justification as a pitched battle to ground right itself. As we have noted, because it merely presupposed right, rather than providing it with valid justification, representationalism, in all its forms, threatened to reduce political authority to a dogmatic "shackle" opposed to any sense of freedom. In so doing, it threatened to render the very core of right itself, its legitimate hold or bindingness over conduct and character, invalid. Hegel thus saw the very concept of right as endangered by the traditional forms of normative justification and their attendant political theories. He thus conceived his own project as a contribution to working out what he called the appropriate "rational form" for the deeply rational content of right because it is only when right possesses this proper form, he argued, that it will be firmly and finally established, that is, it will only then be "justified to free thinking":

> For such thinking does not stop at what is *given*, whether the latter is supported by the external positive authority of the state or of mutual agreement among human beings, or by the authority of inner feeling and the heart and by the testimony of the spirit which immediately concurs with this, but starts out from itself and thereby demands to know itself as united in its innermost being with the truth. (*GW* 14:1, 7)

A genuine science of right is thus demanded, as Hegel understands it, by the fundamental principle of critical thought itself—that we must have the courage to think for ourselves—which Kant proclaimed the core dictum of the Enlightenment. To take the given as the standard of right—and this, as we have seen, is precisely what stands at the core of the project of representationalism—is to cede the very ground of normativity itself.

From Representation to Systematicity

When we reviewed the objects of inquiry of the representational forms of knowledge that Hegel lists in the opening paragraph of the *Encyclopedia*, we left one aside—*Recht*—"right," which is the traditional subject matter, Hegel tells us, of jurisprudence, which in German is called *Rechtswissenschaft*, literally, the "science of right." We shall return to a much more detailed consideration of this central concept in chapter 3, but we can already see that the line of argument that Hegel has mounted against representational forms of knowledge, in general, and the representational forms of traditional normative justification, in particular, requires a profound rethinking of this object and of the methodology that seeks to found it. The pivotal question, then, for Hegel, is what would constitute a nonrepresentational form of *Recht* and, correlatively, what would be a genuine science of right? We have seen that the central problem of representational forms of knowledge in general is that they presuppose both their object and their methodology. We have also seen that, although he rejects their basic justificatory strategies, Hegel affirms the fundamental goals of rationalism and empiricism, namely that the concept of right must be defined and that it must be conceived concretely. What would it mean, then, to begin in political philosophy without taking the nature or the existence of what one was investigating, namely *Recht*, for granted and without a justificatory procedure already in place by which to consider the matter? What would it mean to understand right in a conceptually precise, yet determinate fashion?

Hegel has already shown that to justify the authoritativeness of right requires a type of argumentation that is not beholden to representation, one that, out of fidelity to the principle of critique itself, abjures all presuppositions. Such a science would have to be, in a word, systematic. Of course, with this, we have in hand what amounts to the negative criterion for Hegel's project, and we can now clearly see the methodological imperative that motivated this enterprise, but the question still remains: What would a genuine system of right such as this look like? What would be its distinctive form of normative argumentation?

Systematicity and Normative Justification

As we noted at the beginning of this chapter, it is precisely on this issue that Hegel leaves us with a dilemma: he repeatedly proclaims that what is ultimately distinctive about his science of right is its systematic method, and that it ought to be judged by this standard alone, yet he also acknowledges that, throughout the *Elements of the Philosophy of Right*, he presupposes a familiarity with this kind of scientific procedure and even admits to omitting the precise derivation of each and every detail involved in this project. The dilemma is certainly ironic since, as we have seen, the science of right clearly presupposes a method that is itself committed to taking nothing for granted. Yet, despite this, Hegel does offer students of the *Elements of the Philosophy of Right* several remarks on methodology that, although brief, we can take, together with his rejection of representationalism, as guiding clues to develop an account of systematic normative justification. In this section, then, I use these passages to work out a basic sketch of Hegel's general philosophical methodology, and I then show how this method serves him as a distinctly nonrepresentationalist form of normative justification.

Systematicity and Justification

Hegel's remarks regarding philosophical method define systematic justification in terms of three fundamental and interrelated principles—(1) immanent development, (2) necessary entailment, and (3) retrogressive grounding—and one fundamental precondition—the justification of the systematic standpoint itself. Let us consider each of these elements in turn.

The cornerstone of the systematic form of justification is its commitment to presuppositionlessness. As we have seen, in distinction from representationalism, this means that systematic justification cannot presuppose its object, its content, nor can it presuppose its method, its form. But if neither the subject matter of the science, nor its mode of demonstration can be taken as given, then the justification of each can only be established together. Object and method, content and form, must be inseparably one. The content cannot be taken over and simply unpacked, nor can the method be presupposed and applied to whatever the subject of investigation may be. The epistemic credentials of both must be established together. In philosophical science, Hegel says in the famous "Preface" to the *Elements of the Philosophy of Right*, "the content is essentially bound up with the *form*" (*GW* 14:1, 6).

Systematic justification's commitment to set aside all assumptions thus entails methodological immanence. Its basic task is to suspend all that might serve as preconceptions about both the nature of the object it seeks to examine and the procedures to be employed in justifying it and, instead, to faithfully observe the way in which the matter at issue develops wholly of itself and thus how it itself demands to be thought. Systematic justification, as a general philosophical enterprise, therefore seeks to do nothing other than attend to the immanent conceptual unfolding of its object, for it is only in abiding by this stipulation that dogmatism and skepticism can be avoided—because nothing is taken for granted, nothing is open to the skeptic's trilemma—and, concordantly, form and content can truly be one. As Hegel puts it in the *Elements of the Philosophy of Right*, a science of right must "observe [*zuzusehen*] the matter at issue's own immanent development" (*GPR* §2) and this is the "method whereby the concept, in science, develops itself out of itself and is merely an *immanent* progression and production of its own determinations" (*GPR* §31).

But if, as Hegel argues, the task of philosophical science is to grasp the immanent development of its subject matter, then this development must be intrinsic to the matter itself. It cannot be produced by extrinsic associations. That is to say, for the development of an object to be genuinely immanent, it must be the whole and complete unfolding of the nature of the matter itself; it must be the articulation of its essence. The immanent development of an object is thus the unfolding of the set of properties that make an object what it is; the features that demarcate it from all other things, its "determinations [*Bestimmungen*]." But since these determinations are the essential predicates of the object, their unfolding must correspond to their inherent relationality. Given that these determinations mutually constitute the object, their relations to one another must be that of necessity. That is, since these determinations are mutually and exhaustively implicative, each property must, of necessity, entail the other. The modality of the development thus follows from its immanence. The conceptual elaboration of a matter is the development of one concept into another where the former necessarily entails the latter. As Hegel puts it, the principal concern of philosophical knowledge is "the *necessity* of the concept" (*GPR* §2A).

The commitment to immanent development leads to that of necessary entailment, and this to what is arguably the most innovative and distinctive feature of Hegel's theory of systematic justification: retrogressive grounding. This idea follows out the central implication of presuppositionlessness. Hegel recognizes that to suspend all presuppositions disallows taking the veracity of the object from which one starts for granted, and since observing the immanent unfolding of the object is setting out the complex of properties that makes the object what it is, the line of argumentation involved in this kind of justificatory enterprise cannot follow that of traditional linear derivation. Specifically, the beginning cannot serve, as in conventional forms of justification, as a foundational or noninferential axiom from which further premises or conclusions are to be deduced. Systematic justification, for Hegel, is thus not a conventional foundationalist form of argumentation. But its rejection of classical foundations and the epistemology of intuition does not lead Hegel to affirm that justification is a function solely of the relationships that can be established between various claims or concepts, the central tenet of coherentism. Instead, Hegel's method cuts a clear path between these conventional alternatives.

As we have seen, the hallmark of systematic justification is that it sets forth the immanent and necessary unfolding of its object. What this kind of analysis shows is that the object with which the inquiry begins is comprised of a set of necessary relations between concepts. As mutually necessary and exhaustively implicative, these relations constitute the object in question as what it is. These relations, then, are the ground of the object that they together comprise. Accordingly, the linear progression from the object to the conceptual relations that constitute it is a retrogression into its ground, the origin and truth upon which the object with which we begin depends and from which it arises. In systematic justification, then, to move forward is, in a sense, to move back, and to move back is to secure the non-arbitrary status and veracity of what precedes. Hegel thus refers to the object of science as the "result [*Resultat*]" of that which precedes it: "In philosophical cognition . . . the chief concern is the *necessity* of a concept, and the path by which it has become, as result, [is] its proof and deduction" (*GPR* §2A). The proof structure of systematic demonstration therefore moves from what is in need of justification back into the set of conceptual relations that form the foundation from which its object originates and upon which it continually depends.

Yet an important problem obviously remains here. As it stands, the construction of a system, for Hegel, seems to be little more than the fashioning of a "seamless web" of interdependence. But this model does not, in itself at least, ensure that its members and their interrelations are in any way truth-preserving. That is to say, it looks as though Hegel has advanced a holistic account of knowledge that is open to the classical objection that coherence is not itself a sufficient indicator of truth. A body of knowledge that holds together does not, by virtue of that fact alone, entail that it properly articulates the joints and junctures of reality.

Hegel recognized this crucial problem and, throughout his career, maintained that the standpoint from which the system of reason is to be constructed, the standpoint of systematic knowledge, itself stands in need of justification. He, in fact, devised two distinct epistemic strategies by which to address this issue in the period under investigation here: (1) the phenomenological investigation of the forms of consciousness to show that absolute knowing is the condition for the possibility of all more elementary kinds of knowledge, the project he had undertaken in the *Phenomenology of Spirit* (1807); and (2) the decision simply to think purely, that is, to abstract from anything and everything and for thought thereby to grasp itself in its own simplicity (*Enz. 1817*, §36A).

The first route is obviously well known, though its exact significance is disputed.[8] The second is less familiar, so a word about it is in order: to think purely, to think abstractly, has a twofold sense.

First, it is a disengaging of thought from its entanglement with all that it takes for granted; in this sense, it is a suspension of thought's commitments, whether tacit or explicit, to any and all preconceptions about itself and the world it inhabits.

Second, though it is a withdrawal, it is not an escape into nothing; it not only "abstracts from everything," but, having done this, it "grasps its pure abstraction," namely itself, the activity of thinking, in its "simplicity." Now, given that such thought has set aside the core assumptions of representation, and the centerpiece of these is the presupposition that the knowing subject stands over against the object it seeks to know, Hegel claims that to think purely is not, strictly speaking, a form of knowledge at all. In grasping itself, it does not know itself; rather, it withdraws into itself and exists as nothing other than the mere activity of withdrawal. It is not known, or conceived of; it simply and immediately is.

Hegel therefore concludes that to think purely and abstractly is to think pure being, being in general. A truly presuppositionless system must begin then with the "objective thought" of being, free from any specificity or concreteness of any kind; in other words, a genuine system must begin with the sheer indeterminacy of being.

Now, further investigation of the specifics of these approaches is beyond the scope of the present study, but what is clear is that they both have the same mission: to establish the oneness of thought and being so that the concepts and relations out of which the system is to be fashioned already have their ontological credentials secured; so that, as he puts it, the "determinations of thinking" have the "value and significance of being in and for themselves the ground of everything" (*Enz. 1817*, §17).

Systematic justification thus stands on the terrain cleared and vindicated by this preparatory investigation and, by so doing, its observing of the immanent and necessary unfolding of a subject matter back into its ground is, at its core, a form of what can be called ontological justification, an establishing of the fundamental orders and constitutive processes of being. Systematicity is thus, for Hegel, necessarily and ineliminably metaphysical because anything less would require deriving content representationally from outside the oneness of thought and being. Hegel, in this way, is thus able to capture the core of foundationalism's concern with grasping the nature and truth of reality itself and coherentism's insistence on constitutive relational dependence in a way that avoids the dogmatism of the former and the relativism of the latter.

Taken together, then, the principles of systematic justification and the vindication of the systematic standpoint mean that the warrant of a concept, claim, or belief to be what it purports to be is vindicated if and only if it is shown to be a moment that is either itself the result of a conceptual unfolding of some object or is a moment in a differential relation included in such a progression. The construction of this kind of system is therefore, at the same time, the justification of its constitutive parts.

Systematic Method

To complete our sketch of Hegel's model of systematic justification, we need briefly to turn from its metaphilosophical underpinnings to the actual system itself. We do so not in order to set out its shape and structure, but solely to note the special role that its first part, the Science of Logic, plays in the system as a whole. As we have seen, in order for systematic justification to avoid the threats of dogmatism and skepticism inherent in representational forms of knowledge, it is entitled to assume neither its content, nor any form of argumentation. This means that Hegel's appeals to the necessity of assessing his work in terms of its speculative methodology must refer to the distinctive method that the system itself establishes from within itself. This is one of the fundamental tasks of the first part of the system, the Science of Logic.

Though this is a matter of some debate among scholars, in the Science of Logic Hegel sets forth a fundamental ontology, a genuinely critical metaphysics, that has, as its culmination, an account of the basic structure of systematic method. The placement of the discussion is itself telling. Method is the culmination of the project of the Science of Logic. Its epistemic standing is thus a matter of the way in which it follows from the ontological analyses that precede it. Systematic justification stands or falls not just on its form, but with its metaphysical content. If the critical ontology laid out in the main body of this science remains faithful to the principles of immanent development, necessary entailment, and retrogressive grounding, then, and only then, would it be possible to identify the fundamental rational structure of reality, and the mode of knowing and form of justification appropriate to it would, it follows, be the one that abides by its inherent form. Hence, an account of systematic method must necessarily come, contra the entire tradition of methodological treatises, at the end of such an inquiry, for it is only there that its own authoritativeness is established.

The core line of argument that Hegel develops in the Science of Logic begins with the emptiness of the concept of pure being, for only this is left when all presuppositions have been laid aside. Hegel shows that, if the immanent developmental structure of being is followed, it proves to be nothing other than what he calls "actuality [*Wirklichkeit*]," the set of all entities that are constituted in and through their complete, necessary, and reciprocal causal interaction with one another. Crucially, he then argues that this thoroughgoing relationality is itself produced by an immanent generative process. This process is the movement of self-differentiation. All objects come to be what they are through self-negation, that is to say, all entities attain their own self-identity by othering themselves, and, in and through this negation, come finally to be themselves. Hegel calls this movement the concept (*Begriff*). When this logical process is fully and exhaustively differentiated, that is, when it is no longer just a process, but when its complete conceptual structure has been explicated, and thus fully actualized, it is, he says, the idea (*Idee*). Hegel's central claim in the Science of Logic, and in the core of his system as a whole, is thus that the actualized movement of self-differentiation, the idea, is the absolute ground and truth of being, the foundation of all objects and relations. The immanent development of being thus necessarily entails the idea as its retrogressive ground.

Now, having demonstrated this thesis about the fundamental nature of reality, Hegel turns, at the end of this first part of the system, to the issue of method (*Enz. 1817*, §§183–91, esp. 185–90). He argues there that the concept exhibits a consistent pattern of generative development: from immediate abstract identity to immanent differentiation and, from this, this negation necessarily negating itself, to its deeper, more concrete fulfillment. But since this has proven to be the very fundamental ontological structure of being itself, this pattern is not only the governing form in and through which all things come to be what they are, but it must at the same time be the method, the way of knowing, that is true to the process of determination inherent within being itself. The structure of the concept as generative process is the proper structure of knowledge itself. Hegel thus concludes that the proper method of philosophical argumentation—if it is not to be, as it is in representational forms of knowledge, a ready-made procedure applied to each and every object from without—must be this form of immanent development: all things become what they are, become themselves, in and through the movement of determinate negation. To be, then, is to be a moment in the process of immanent differentiation; it is to be part of the process of becoming-other whereby all things come to be determinate. Accordingly, showing something to be such a moment is thus to give it its proper justification, the demonstration of its true standing, of its standing in the movement of actualization that is the concept. This process, of course, is the infamous "higher dialectic of the concept," which consists, Hegel tells us, "in producing and seizing the determination not merely as an opposite and restriction, but as the *positive* content and result that it [the dialectic of the concept] contains as that whereby it is alone a *development* and immanent progression" (*GPR* §31A).

Obviously, much more would need to be said in order to offer a full interpretation and defense of Hegel's account of method here, but this much suffices to show that the distinctive concern of the Science of Logic is not just ontological, but ultimately epistemological, for what the first part of the system establishes is that the true way of knowing, the way of knowing things in their truth, is nothing other than the process of development that is proper to being itself, and this is to grasp the rationality, the dialectic of the concept, within all that is. It follows that the other parts of the system, the Philosophies of Nature and of Spirit, the latter of which the *Philosophy of Right* is a part, are properly subordinate to the Science of Logic, since it is only insofar as they discern the movement of the concept, the movement set out and established by the Logic, as the process constitutive of their own distinct domains, that their claims and concepts are able to stand vindicated.[9] The fundamental task of philosophical knowledge, for Hegel, is thus to grasp the movement of the dialectic as the immanent process whereby any and all objects come to be determinate, and that is, as Hegel puts it, "to bring to consciousness the matter's own work of reason" (*GPR* §31A).

Systematicity and Normativity

With this account of systematic justification in hand, we can now come to the second of our original questions: How is the systematic method of argumentation able to serve as a form of normative justification?

As we have seen, the hallmark of systematic justification is its rejection of representationalism and the commitment to the principles of immanence, necessity, and retrogressive grounding that this entails. Furthermore, we saw Hegel argue that the pattern that the process of immanent development exhibits is that of the self-differentiating movement of the concept as it actualizes itself into the idea. Systematic justification, then, is attending to the immanent and necessary conceptual unfolding of an object back into its ground where this development proves to be fundamentally dialectical. The question now before us is thus how this unique method is able to vindicate the authoritativeness of a claim with respect to action or a form of life. That is to say, how can the dialectic of the concept establish normative warrant?

The core of Hegel's answer to this question is the necessary relationship that he contends exists between the concepts of freedom and right. Now we shall, of course, treat both of these concepts in much more detail in the chapters that follow, but we need to note here that Hegel's examination of the concept of right takes the concept of freedom as its starting point because it is seeking to set forth a justification of right itself, and insofar as right is claimed to be authoritative with respect to the conduct and character of free agents, then the dictates of the systematic method require that right be shown to follow—immanently, of necessity, and as the ground of—the concept of freedom. The basic shape of Hegel's broader argument regarding this relationship becomes clear by examining the first two paragraphs of the *Philosophy of Right*. To do so, we begin by returning, once again, to the problem of representation.

Representational forms of knowledge, we recall, take the object of their inquiry—an image borne originally from intuition, but generalized by the power of representation—for granted. To treat right as a representational object would be to take it either as the natural law of rationalism or the feeling, sentiment, or tradition of empiricism. Down both of these paths, as we have seen, lie dogmatism and the skeptic's trilemma. A truly critical account of right must be presuppositionless. It must set aside the conceptions offered by intellectual and sensible intuition and, instead, begin with nothing other than the pure concept of right itself. But what exactly is this?

Hegel begins the *Philosophy of Right* with a decisive, though stark, statement that responds to this fundamental question: "The philosophical science of right has the idea [*Idee*] of right, the concept of right and its actualization [*Verwirklichung*], for its object" (*GPR* §1). Now, if we were to read this proposition by employing the standard definitions of its principal terms, we would conclude that the kind of philosophical inquiry being proposed here is concerned with the ultimate exemplar of right, that which is common to all individual rightful acts, dispositions, and states of affairs, and with the instantiations of this generality in particular cases. Such an interpretation would construe Hegel's project as a form of classical natural law, presupposing right as a transcendent moral order. But this, of course, is not what the idea of right is. But neither is it merely an empirical representation, an expression of subjective desire. Both of these readings would fall prey to representationalism. Hegel is instead employing the central terms here in the technical sense that we saw him develop in the Science of Logic, and this means that what is properly at stake in the science of right, for him, is something quite different than either of these ready-made conceptions.

Idea, for Hegel, we recall, denotes the fully differentiated concrete realization of the concept. Accordingly, the idea of right refers to the culmination of a process whereby the complete relational actuality of right—a world of authoritative social institutions and practices—is set forth. The proper object of the science of right is thus not a pre-given transcendent moral order, nor a ready-made feeling, sentiment, or tradition, but a set of interrelated normative social and political structures. The substance of the work to follow, then, that is, the substance of the *Philosophy of Right* itself, is to unfold the immanent and necessary moments of this object. The "concept of right and its actualization" thus designates the generative movement of self-differentiation, the "higher dialectic," whereby the interdependent domain of right is constituted and its standing as the ground of all that precedes it is vindicated. The object of the science of right, then, is not simply the result of this process, the constituted domain of normativity, but the conceptual progression of which this normative whole proves to be the result. In other words, the object of the science of right is the unfolding of the concept of right from its abstract immediacy through its immanent self-negation whereby it comes into its own as a concrete whole.

Hegel notes the special sense in which the notions of concept and idea are being employed here in the Remark to this opening paragraph:

> Philosophy has to do with ideas and therefore not with what are commonly called *mere concepts*. On the contrary, it exposes the latter as one-sided and untruthful, and that it is the concept alone (not what is so often called by that name, but which is merely an abstract determination of the understanding) that has actuality, and in such a way that it gives actuality to itself. (*GPR* §1A)

The task of the science of right is thus rigorously to observe the immanent development of the pure concept of right into its interdependent whole, which is to say, its complete actualization, the concept become actualized as idea, the way that "it gives actuality to itself." But how does this in any way establish the authoritativeness of right itself?

Hegel's answer to this question comes in the second paragraph of the work. "The science of right," he reminds us, "is a *part of philosophy*" (*GPR* §2). From this simple proposition, he draws two implications that stand at the very core of the project of the *Philosophy of Right*. The *first*, as we have already noted, is that for the science of right to be a genuinely philosophical, as opposed to a representational, form of inquiry, it must commit itself, as he puts it here, "to observe the matter at issue's own immanent development" (*GPR* §2). The method of a philosophical science of right must be immanent, necessary, and retrogressive; in a word, systematic.

The *second* implication is the more relevant one for our present purposes:

> As a part, it [the science of right] has a determinate *starting point*, which is the *result* and truth of what *preceded* it, and what preceded it constitutes the so-called *proof* of that result. Hence, the concept of right, so far as its *becoming* is concerned, falls outside the science of right; its deduction is presupposed here and is to be taken as *given*. (*GPR* §2)

Like the first paragraph, this passage initially appears deeply puzzling, if not simply misleading. It seems to suggest that the science of right presupposes its object, the concept of right. We, of course, know that this can't be the case, but what exactly does it mean to say that the "proof [*Beweis*]" of the core concept of the science "falls outside" the science itself? How can a science where the justification of right is not itself a part of the science be a form of systematic normative justification?

The key here is the term "part [*Teil*]." Hegel's claim is that the science of right is a distinctly philosophical endeavor and, as such, it must abide by the systematic principles of immanence, necessity, and retrogressive grounding. But, as a part, it is not itself the whole of philosophical science. It is a distinct science within a broader system. This means that the justification of the object whose immanent development the philosophical science of right seeks to observe must necessarily precede this specific science. The "becoming [*Werden*]" of the concept of right—by which Hegel means its genesis as a moment within the immanent and necessary unfolding of a more basic concept—"falls outside" the science of right. But since this development of right from a more basic concept is, in systematic justification, as we have seen, the proof of its ontological and epistemological standing, then the justification of right itself is, strictly speaking, not what is at issue in the science of right proper. How then are we to understand the science of right in relation to the justification of its object?

Hegel's crucial thesis, the one upon which the entire normative character of the argument of the *Philosophy of Right* hinges, is that the justification of the concept of right consists in its being shown to be the immanent and necessary ground—the result or truth, as Hegel would say—of the more basic, and thus less determinate, concept of freedom. That is to say, unfolding the essential determinations of freedom shows that it is what it is only by virtue of the concept of right. Right, then, is the condition of the possibility of freedom. The content of these claims, of course, needs to be unpacked, and we shall turn to their substance in the chapters that follow, but the issue at present is the fundamental structure of this kind of argumentation: How is it able to establish the authoritativeness of right itself and how can this authoritativeness, in turn, be said to flow to the more concrete determinations of right, its actualization?

The systematic method proves decisive here, for it is only by following its strictures that the normative standing of right and its concrete determinations can be justified in a way that avoids the dangers of skepticism. The nerve of Hegel's systematic justification of the concept of right is that it is the result of the immanent and necessary unfolding of the essential determinations of freedom and thus is its ground. As such, right is not only essential to being free, but it has binding authority over all forms of free acting. Under representational forms of knowledge, it is simply taken for granted that right—whether it is conceived as a transcendent moral order, as in rationalist Enlightened Absolutism, or as the weight of tradition and desire, as in empiricist Conservatism and Romanticism—possesses legitimate authority over conduct and character. Such approaches thereby render the relationship that stands at the very core of the problem of normativity vulnerable to arbitrariness, regressivity, or vicious circularity. Systematic justification, on the contrary, is able to show that right is not only one of the essential determinations discovered in the unfolding of freedom, it is the concrete existence, the necessary embodiment, through which human striving is able to be genuinely free. But if being free is made possible by right itself, then this concept and its further, more concrete, determinations possess legitimate binding authority with respect to free actions and forms of life because they have proved to be the retrogressive ground of freedom itself. The normativity that is right thus flows from its being what ultimately constitutes freedom itself, or what we shall call, following Hegel, the objectivity of freedom: "the system of right is the realm of actualized freedom" (*GPR* §4).

Given this interpretation of Hegel's project, the philosophical science of right is thus indeed defined by its distinctive systematic methodology, its "philosophical manner of progressing from one matter to another and of conducting a scientific proof, the speculative way of knowing in general" (*GW* 14:1, 5). And we have seen that this is nothing less than its commitment, negatively, to presuppositionlessness, the rejection of representationalism, and positively, to immanence, necessity, and retrogressive grounding, to the "higher dialectic of the concept." The critique of representationalism allowed Hegel to move beyond the confines of the conceptual space of late eighteenth and early nineteenth-century German political thought and its traditional forms of justification and to outflank the Agrippan challenge that lurked behind these boundaries. But it was by bringing the demands of immanence, necessity, and retrogressive grounding to bear on the concept of freedom that he was able to open a decisively new pathway for thinking and justifying normativity itself. The object of the science of right is the "concept of right and its actualization," the idea of right, and this is nothing other than the immanent and necessary unfolding of right as the enabling institutional embodiment of freedom. The normative standing of a concept, principle, institution, or practice thus derives, in Hegel's account, from its being shown to be a necessary determination, and this means a necessary actualization, of freedom. In this way, one can claim that the fundamental thesis of Hegel's philosophical science of right is that systematicity is the only form of argumentation that is truly capable of fulfilling the task of normative justification. This method, in turn, places the essential relationship between freedom and right at the very heart of political philosophy in a truly unique fashion where the nature of the latter flows directly from the nature of the former. The intricacies of that perplexing claim will be our guiding concern in the next two chapters.

Chapter 2

✦

Freedom

> *Right* is any existence in general that is the *existence* of the *free will*.
> Right is therefore in general freedom, as idea.
>
> —Hegel, *GPR* §29

This thesis expresses the core tenet of Hegel's science of right: right is any structure that embodies freedom. But what precisely does this mean? Answering this fundamental question is the principal task of this and the next chapter. Together they set forth an interpretation of Hegel's general theory of practical normativity by examining his systematic accounts of freedom and right. More specifically, they show how the method of normative justification detailed in chapter 1 is employed by Hegel to demonstrate that the complete unfolding of the concept of freedom—that is, in Hegel's technical formulation, freedom as idea—necessarily entails the concept of right as, at once, its result and ground.

The present chapter examines the basic elements of Hegel's theory of freedom. Central to Hegel's account is the concept of individuality. Individuality, Hegel contends, is the ontological structure that captures the distinctive activity of autonomous action, and he defines it as the integration of the will's universality and its particularity. As we shall see, to make sense of this concept requires unpacking Hegel's broader theory of practical agency, specifically his account of moral psychology and his treatment of the problem of reflection and its proper measure. This, in turn, will lead us to what is clearly the central issue of Hegel's science of right, the account of the objectivity or actuality of freedom, the deduction of the concept of right, the order that Hegel calls Objective Spirit. Establishing this fundamental relationship between freedom and objectivity will allow us to see that self-determination is not simply a matter of personal freedom, the so-called liberty of the individual, but has to do with something more. Objective freedom ultimately denotes, for Hegel, the processes by which social and political institutions establish and govern the framework of rules, practices, and policies that comprise a just society. It is through these conditions, in turn, that individuals and groups are enabled themselves to be genuinely self-governing. The autonomy of the individual, we could thus say, flows, for Hegel, from the autonomy of institutions.

Freedom, Representation, and Systematicity: Spirit and the Will (*GPR* §4; *Enz. 1817*, §§300–306)

Hegel begins the deduction of right—which, as we noted at the end of the previous chapter, must of necessity fall outside the science of right proper and, accordingly, appears in the "Introduction" to the *Elements of the Philosophy of Right* as well as in corresponding sections of the *Encyclopedia*—by locating it within the system of philosophical sciences more generally:

> The basis of right is, in general, the *spiritual* and its precise location and point of departure is the *will*; the will is *free*, so that freedom constitutes its substance and determination and the system of right is the realm of actualized freedom, the world of spirit produced from within itself as a second nature. (*GPR* §4)

Following the claim at *GPR* §2—that the science of right is itself part of the broader system of philosophical sciences—Hegel tells us here that the object of the philosophical science of right, its subject matter, namely the concept of right itself, is a moment in the system as a whole. Right belongs to *neither* of the first two divisions of the system, neither to the Science of Logic nor to the Philosophy of Nature—it is not the idea in itself, in its conceptual abstractness (Logic), nor the idea in its otherness, in its determinacy (Nature)—but rather it belongs properly to the Philosophy of Spirit and, more specifically, to the concept of the will and to the will as free: "the system of right is the realm of actualized freedom."

Having introduced this relationship, Hegel immediately invokes the distinction whose methodological significance we have seen is so crucial for him—namely, the distinction between representation and systematicity and their attendant forms of justification—and he applies it here to the notion of freedom.

Hegel begins with the rationalist theory. In the Remark to *GPR* §4, he notes that the will has been defined as free and proven to be so by appeals to "feelings and appearances" such as remorse, guilt, or moral sentiment of any kind. All such sentiments presuppose that their bearer is capable of complying with them or of choosing to do otherwise; hence, to have such feelings requires possessing a will that is free. But Hegel is quite clear that this type of justification of the will and of its determination as free is wholly derived ("extracted from") from representation and, as such, is thus vulnerable to the charges of skepticism. The alternative empiricist approach—as he puts it, "simply to adhere to the notion that freedom is *given* as a *fact* of consciousness in which we must simply *believe*" (*GPR* §4A)—is no better. Freedom here is taken to be an undeniable, incontrovertible datum that demands our attestation. In presupposing freedom, both strategies thus leave the will and its nature open to skeptical challenge and, in doing so, these representational justifications of freedom threaten the very project of a truly rational account of right.

Now, despite the fact that they differ over the justificatory grounds of freedom, both the rationalist and the empiricist approaches actually share, for Hegel, a common representation of the will and of what it means for it to be free.[1] In its most basic terms, the will is assumed by both to be a capacity to step back and consider a range of options—natural or artificial, desirable or not—and to select among them. The rationalist takes this power to be what being a bearer of moral sentiments presupposes, while the empiricist assumes this ability as a sheer given. But, more deeply, this representational conception of the will is also committed to a view about the nature of agency itself. Specifically, both the rationalist and empiricist hold that desires, beliefs, or intentions—that is, all forms of subjective attitudes or position-takings—cause actions and thereby stand as the purpose that the action fulfills. But, as the action's cause, they are taken to remain separable from the act itself. Desires, beliefs, and intentions are thus, in this implicit ontology, fundamentally mental states that can exist solely in the mind of the agent without necessarily being realized. The representationalist model of the will thus assumes a theory of action where the domain of the mental, the inner, is ontologically separable from the natural, the outer.

We will come back to this conception of freedom along with its inherent contradictions, which Hegel famously refers to as *Willkür* (choice), in the account of the systematic nature of freedom that we will explore later in this chapter, but it is worth noting here that this same representationalist approach to freedom actually underpins the dominant contemporary interpretations of Hegel's own theory of freedom. Three paradigms, in particular, define the current terrain.[2] The discredited, but still widely held view, is the *conventionalist interpretation*, which contends that to be free, for Hegel, is to act in accord with the mores and conventions of the society within which one finds one's self.[3] The *self-actualization interpretation*, which joins Hegel to a long line of thought that derives social and political philosophy from some ultimate intrinsic value, holds freedom itself to be the supreme value that must be taken as basic and thus as the measure against which the worth of institutions and practices is to be assessed.[4] Finally, the more recent *historicist interpretation* takes freedom to be the supreme normative concept of a specific historical worldview, namely, modernity, in which all are held to be individual actors, responsible for their doings and thus free, a worldview whose authority derives from its having successfully surmounted the seemingly intractable problems inherent in earlier shared forms of life.[5] Yet despite the very real differences between these accounts, they nonetheless all conceive of freedom, *at least minimally*, as the power of choice with all that that entails, and they take this ability to be either an intrinsic good (as in the self-actualization interpretation) or historically given (as in the conventionalist and historicist readings).[6] As such, these paradigms, albeit unknowingly, offer accounts of Hegel's theory of freedom that render it vulnerable precisely to the very skeptical challenges against which he sought to safeguard it.

Hegel's response to the rationalist and empiricist approaches of his day is thus just as applicable to the current discussion: "The deduction *that* the will is free and *what* the will and freedom are . . . takes place only within the interconnections [*Zusammenhange*] of the whole" (*GPR* §4A). That the will is free, and what that and even willing itself mean, requires demonstration in order to secure them against the skeptics' critiques and, as we saw in the previous chapter, for this to succeed, any such demonstration must abide by the strictures of the systematic form of justification. As Hegel clearly notes at *GPR* §4 regarding the concept of right, this means nothing less than showing how the concept of the will, even in the sense of *Willkür*, immanently and necessarily follows from the unfolding of the concept of spirit. So, a properly systematic account of freedom must thus begin with the question: What is spirit (*Geist*)?

Hegel defines *Geist*, in its most general terms, at *Enz. 1817*, §302, as a distinctive kind of process: manifestation (*Manifestation*).[7] For Hegel, manifestation denotes the movement of the concept becoming actual, becoming itself, but not just as it develops logically, but in its determinacy, and that is in and through its becoming nature. Nature is thus, as he says at *Enz. 1817*, §300, spirit's presupposition (*Voraussetzung*), and spirit proves to be nature's truth (*Wahrheit*). Now, from our examination of the rudiments of Hegel's ontology in the previous chapter, we know that this means that spirit is the concept that immanently and necessarily follows from the concept of nature—nature is thus spirit's presupposition—and that spirit is the retrogressive ground—the truth—of nature. But a complete account of the complex relationship between spirit and nature in Hegel's thought is, of course, beyond the parameters of the present study. For our purposes here, three things are important to note.

The first is that, for Hegel, as a process of manifestation, spirit is not what is revealed; it is not the thing, the something (*Etwas*), that is manifested or displayed; rather, it is solely the process of disclosure, the process of manifestation, itself (see *Enz. 1817*, §302). It ultimately reveals only and wholly itself, the movement of revealing. So, spirit is not a being among other beings. It is not God or Man, whether the individual or society as a whole. Instead, spirit is the generative ontological process whereby all things, all beings, come to be what they are as this is determined not just abstractly (as the Idea in the Science of Logic is), nor simply in the world itself (as life in the Philosophy of Nature is), but as this process comes into its own, as it comes to be what it is. And this means that spirit is the Idea's othering of itself *as* nature, that is, as a movement that is endemic to the natural realm, but not itself simply a natural process.

This brings us to the second point. If spirit is the process of manifestation whereby all things come to be what they are, and if this process is natural, but not simply equivalent to any natural process, then its relationship to nature can be understood neither in terms of dualistic opposition, nor even as a form of compatibilism.[8] Spirit, for Hegel, clearly does not stand over against nature, but its movement is not merely compatible with the domain of natural events and processes either. Spirit is not threatened by the causal determinacy of nature because, as Hegel shows in the Philosophy of Nature, nature itself is not fundamentally deterministic. But this doesn't simply allow, as compatibilism usually holds, for an underdetermined space within which spirit can operate. Rather, Hegel's claim is that spirit's revelatoriness is itself a natural process, yet unlike other natural processes, spirit is marked by a distinctive kind of self-relation. Spirit is characteristic of organisms that are sufficiently complex so as to be able to register their interaction or encountering of other natural beings or the natural environment as a whole.[9] What is registered in such beings, at least at the most basic level, according to Hegel, is the unity of the organism's own physiology, its corporeality, the complex of feelings and sensations that arise in and through the organism's interaction with its surrounding environment. It is thus this rudimentary form of self-relation that differentiates the process of spirit as manifestation from all other natural processes. It follows from this that what is at issue in the Philosophy of Spirit as a whole, for Hegel, is the nature of the different forms of this self-relation as a process of manifestation and as this is mediated in, through, and as the natural environment.

To move now to the third point, we can see that it is precisely this question—of the forms of self-relation of the movement of spirit in, through, and as the natural world—that dictates the structure of this domain of philosophical sciences—the Philosophy of Spirit—as Hegel sets this out at *Enz. 1817*, §§305–6:

(a) *Subjective Spirit*: an account of the movement of manifestation that is spirit insofar as it simply finds (*Vorfinden*) the world of nature before it, that is, as merely presupposed; accordingly, as revealing, subjective spirit transforms nature into ideality, that is, into something known (Theoretical Spirit = Intelligence) and, ultimately, into something that moves it to act in, with, and upon this world (Practical Spirit = Will): *Enz. 1817*, §§307–99; see also, *GPR* §4A.
(b) *Objective Spirit*: an account of the movement of spirit as it produces or constructs (*Erzeugen*) the world of nature now as a world of its own fashioning and through which it is able to come into a practical self-relation, or what Hegel calls a second nature, as distinct from the first nature that subjective spirit encounters: *Enz. 1817*, §§400–452.
(c) *Absolute Spirit*: an account of the movement that is spirit fully and completely at one with itself, fully and completely in self-relation, knowing itself as such and thereby attaining its freedom (*Befreyung*), its subjective and objective moments completely and wholly integrated and presented as such in the cultural practices of art, religion, and philosophy: *Enz. 1817*, §§453–77.

So when Hegel tells us that the "precise location and point of departure" for the concept of right within the system of philosophical sciences is the will, and furthermore, when he maintains that the will is, conceptually, the most fully developed form of subjective spirit, he is saying, although the interpretation being proposed here is certainly controversial, that the will is a natural process of disclosure or expression characteristic of organisms that bear a relation to themselves in and through their registering and interacting with their surrounding environment. As we saw above, in its most elementary form, this self-relation is nothing more than a being's felt sense of its own corporeal integrity. In its more advanced configurations, it is the epistemic grasping of the features of the natural world via an organism's sensations, images, and concepts. But in its most developed form, Hegel argues, the movement of manifestation that is subjective spirit shows itself not to be defined solely by a cognitive, but rather by a practical self-relation: instead of grasping its environment through sensations, images, and concepts, the organism's defining activity is its integrating of these into its determining (*Bestimmen*, *Enz. 1817*, §386) of itself by setting ends for it to pursue: "its [the subjective spirit's] determinations are ends [*Zwecke*]; it is free will" (*Enz. 1817*, §387).

Accordingly, the systematic account of the will shows that the will is not fundamentally, as the representationalist conception contends, a power to consider and select among a range of options. Which is not to say, as we shall see, that the capacity to abstract from natural determinations and consider them as options is not an element of what the will is. Rather, Hegel's claim is that the will, understood at its most fundamental level, is necessarily a movement defined uniquely by a self-relation mediated in and through and as the natural environment. Specifically, Hegel's account holds that, again at this fundamental level, insofar as actions are thoroughly natural processes, they are not caused by an inner mental disposition. Rather, actions express or make ends or purposes manifest. These ends are immanent within the action itself, guiding and directing conduct wholly from within. In this sense, the ends or purposes are—that is, they exist as purposes, as ends—only insofar as they are being made manifest, only insofar as they are being posited, striven after, in some fashion or other.[10] The will, then, as the core of what Hegel calls "practical spirit," is not the instrument of some mental cause, nor is it a causal power independent unto itself. Rather, it is nothing other than the embodiment of the process of the setting and pursuing of ends and purposes. The will literally is nothing other than the activity of determining. As such, it is appropriate to say, for Hegel, that the will is more properly understood as the activity in which and through which the ends and purposes it bears within itself are made manifest and, in their most determinate sense, are realized.

Having now distinguished the systematic from the representational conception of freedom, we must examine freedom's basic underlying structure more carefully.[11]

The Ontological Structure of Freedom: Individuality (*GPR* §§5–7)

As we have seen, the core of Hegel's account of freedom is that actions are a distinctive kind of natural event in that they reveal or express the purposes that intrinsically guide or direct them. It is in this sense that this natural event is also, properly speaking, spiritual. Now, for an act to be not only expressive in this sense, but genuinely free as well, Hegel contends that it must meet two conditions:

(a) *Self-Determination Condition*: the end that is expressed must be pursued in such a way that the agent, in and through this act, is self-determining; and
(b) *Objectivity Condition*: the expression of the end must result in the end's becoming actual, that is, the purpose pursued by the act must become objective.

These conditions are reciprocal. A truly self-governing act is only possible insofar as its end becomes actual, and a result and an end becomes genuinely actual to the extent that it enables the agent pursuing it to be self-determining. Together these conditions constitute the necessary and sufficient conditions of freedom itself.[12] The self-determination condition will be the concern of the present chapter, while the objectivity condition will be examined in the following chapter.

Now, as we noted above, Hegel claims that the key to how the will can be, at once, self-determining and objective is the logical structure of individuality, or *Einzelnheit* (*GPR* §7; see also, *Enz. 1817*, §399), and he defines individuality, as we said, as the integration of the will's universality and its particularity. But what exactly does this mean?

As a logical category, individuality is, for Hegel, a determination of both thought and being and it denotes, in particular, the completion of the process of something coming to be what it is, its becoming actual (see *Enz. 1817*, §114). Recall that the central defining claim of the ontology set forth in the Science of Logic is that everything that is comes to be what it is through self-negation, the process of self-differentiation. Hegel calls this movement the concept (*Begriff*) and its culmination, the idea (*Idee*). If we now examine this account further, we find Hegel arguing that the concept-forms of universality, particularity, and individuality elaborate the basic structure of this process: the universality of the concept is its minimal, abstract identity, its bare self-relation, while its particularity is its concrete differentiation, its becoming-other than its simple self-identity, and its individuality marks the culmination of this movement wherein the identity of the concept is completed, brought into its own, precisely in and through its particularization (see *Enz. 1817*, §§112–14). As such, individuality is not, Hegel insists, as representational forms of knowledge would have it, the simple immediacy of an existing entity, a mere this, but rather, it is the unity of the process of determination, of something coming into its own (see *GPR* §7A).

The will's *universality*, its basic identity or abstract self-relation, is its ability to abstract or withdraw itself from any kind of determination that it may find itself in, whether natural (e.g., needs, desire, or inclinations) or artificial (e.g., rules or traditions), so that it is, in and by this withdrawal, immediately and wholly with itself (*GPR* §5). Willing's *particularity*, its immanent self-differentiation, is its positing of something, again be it natural or conventional, as its aim or as the purpose that it is pursuing (*GPR* §6). And finally, the *individuality* of willing consists in the integration of its universality and particularity: to will is to posit and strive after something as an end where, in and through such activity, the agent is, at once, in control and fulfilled, that is, self-related (*GPR* §7; see also, *Enz. 1817*, §388).[13]

Hence, in order to understand how individuality captures the nature of the distinctive form of manifestation that is willing, we must work out exactly what it means to say that the individuality of willing is the integration of its universality and its particularity. Hegel's definition, though admittedly dense in its formulation, is nonetheless instructive:

> The will is the unity of both these moments: *particularity* reflected *into itself* and thereby brought back [*zurückgeführt*] to *universality*—*individuality*; the *self-determination* of the I: it posits itself as the negative of itself, namely as *determinate*, *restricted* and is with itself [*bei sich*], i.e., it remains in its *identity with itself* and universality, and in the determination, it binds itself together with itself. (*GPR* §7)

The individuality of willing is said here to lie in two interrelated, but distinct moments: (a) the reflection of particularity into itself; and (b) this reflection bringing the will back to its universality, that is, to its self-relation. It will be useful to begin our examination of this structure by briefly outlining each moment before we turn to a more sustained examination of Hegel's treatment of each of these claims.

As we said above, the particularity of the activity of willing, for Hegel, is its positing of something or resolving on something, whether natural or artificial, as the end or goal that it seeks to pursue and thus as the purpose that it seeks to express (see *GPR* §6). Hence, the strategy that Hegel pursues in order to address the question at hand is to undertake an investigation of the motivational structure of such expressivity. Specifically, he traces action back to its roots in natural determinations—the moral psychology of feelings, drives, inclinations, and passions—and shows how these affective elements move the will to act. He rejects the largely Platonic tradition that posits a dualism between reason and the domain of the natural, the sensuous realm of feeling, emotion, and desire, developing instead an integrated account of the role of affectivity in willing generally and in its rational self-determination, in particular.

The core of Hegel's analysis revolves around the claim that for any natural affectivity to become motivational, it must be incorporated by the will as a moment of its own self-determination. This, Hegel contends, requires nothing less than the introduction of reflection and, with it, a principle of judgment, a criterion or measure of genuinely free action. The will, for Hegel, is thus not a blind force, but a process that is necessarily under the guidance of thought. To be genuinely free requires the integration of the cognitive, the affective, and the volitional, the unity of what Hegel calls theoretical and practical spirit.[14] The question that stands at the heart of Hegel's account thus clearly becomes what is the appropriate criterion, the proper measure, by which the will is able to be genuinely self-determining in and through its expressivity. That is, how is reflection of the will's particularity into itself able to bring the will back to itself, to its universality, to its fundamental self-relation?

The argument Hegel sets out in response to this question is extremely intricate and nuanced and, as such, will require careful reconstruction, but its basic trajectory is nonetheless legible: for natural affections to be moments of the will's own self-determination, for them to be incorporated into the will as its own motivational wellsprings, their authoritativeness, their rightness, which is to say their justification as opposed simply to their motivational role, must be established by appeal to the principle that defines the very nature of the will itself, that is, by appeal to the principle of autonomy. In order to do this, Hegel argues, the will must, through reflection, posit itself as its own end and express its affections by making freedom itself objective, by making autonomy real. In so doing, the will satisfies the conditions of self-determination and objectivity and thereby moves from freedom as concept to freedom as idea.

With this outline in hand, we can examine the claims about particularity and reflection more closely. We begin, following Hegel's own discussion, with natural particularity in its most elemental form: practical feeling.[15]

The Motivational Structure of Freedom: Practical Feeling, Drive, and Passion (*Enz. 1817*, §§389–95)

Practical feeling, for Hegel, denotes the most rudimentary kind of moral intuition, the spontaneous affective appraisal whereby an agent finds certain sorts of deeds or principles to be good or bad. It is a sense of sympathy or fairness, a feeling, as Hegel puts it, that is lodged in the "heart" (*Enz. 1817*, §390A) from which our conduct and character spring and from which they take their bearings. Human action, in the end, is always, for Hegel, an expression of some form of practical feeling. But as a feeling, it is something that an agent simply finds within herself. To have a sense of what is right is a natural sensation, a mere particularity, and thus it is, fundamentally, a contingent determination, an intuition that merely happens to arise in one's inner being. As such, it can possess no justificatory power. That is, moral sentiment cannot, of itself, establish the rightness of any principle or act. Hegel consistently rejects any form of an "ethics of feeling" because this inevitably leads, he claims, to some kind of moral hedonism and thus to bondage of the will. And yet, he contends, the expressivity of the will, precisely as an autonomous activity, finds its most elementary wellspring in just this kind of normative affectivity. How, then, is such particularity capable of engendering genuinely self-determining volition? The answer lies, as we shall see, in how it becomes reflected into itself.

Hegel introduces the concept of feeling (*Gefühl*) in the context of his account of human cognition, or what he calls intelligence in the section of Subjective Spirit in the *Encyclopedia* devoted to this issue: "Theoretical Spirit." It is, he says, the matter that sentient organisms, in general, register at the most elementary level of perceptual awareness (see *Enz. 1817*, §369). In this period, Hegel draws no sharp distinction between the simple immediacy of sensation (*Empfindung*) and feeling. Both denote, for him, the passively received, noncognitive intuition—that which is merely found or felt—that, in turn, serves as the material for higher-order mental processes. What distinguishes *practical* feeling from *theoretical* feeling is thus not its affectivity, but rather its intrinsic normativity: practical feelings are always marked by an "ought [*Sollen*]," Hegel says, that no other form of sensuous intuition displays (*Enz. 1817*, §391). To feel cold is to register the fact of that bodily condition, but to have a sense of what is right—for instance, to have a feeling for sociability or justice—is already to experience such a state of affairs as demanding to be realized. Practical feelings are thus inherently and ineliminably imperative.

Normativity thus first appears in Hegel's account as a distinctive feature of practical feeling. And, as such, it is a sheer givenness that is necessitated, not by any appeal to brute fact, but by the immanent conceptual unfolding of the concept of feeling itself. To perceive is not simply to register sensation regarding existent states of affairs. It is also to register higher-order aspirational affects, senses of what ought and what ought not to be. However, it is important to note here—and it is a point that we shall develop in the course of the analyses that follow—that the normative character of practical feelings, while central to the account of volitional motivation, is not sufficient of itself, according to Hegel, to establish its own authoritativeness. Practical feeling is not its own warrant; such feelings simply present themselves, and this is what distinguishes them, as making such claims. Establishing their entitlement to this claim, the question of normative justification itself, the question of right, as Hegel shows, is ultimately a matter of the will and its conditions of self-determination and objectivity. For now, though, we will pursue Hegel's immanent analysis of feeling as motivational to show precisely where and how the issue of justification emerges within that account.

Hegel traces the origin of the normative nature of practical feelings to a discord between their form and their content. As normative, the content of such feelings is always universal and necessary, while its form, as being held in one's heart, is particular and contingent. As Hegel puts it, insofar as the feeling, precisely and exclusively as a subjective intuition, remains merely "in relation to determinacy," it can be nothing other than wholly subjective, transient, and superficial, nothing more than a "*feeling* of the *pleasant* or the *unpleasant*" (*Enz. 1817*, §391). Now, in such a condition, the will, as the human capacity to govern its conduct, is confronted by the normative givenness of practical feeling, and since the very nature of willing is to be self-determining, this already frames willing as an inherent contradiction: the natural particularity of willing, its being affected by practical feeling, stands opposed to its universality, its ability to withdraw itself from any and all encumbrances and stand in pure self-relation. Hegel thus concludes that the immediacy of practical feeling constitutes a "negation" (*Enz. 1817*, §392) of the will's essential nature.

Hegel contends that it is the ought-character of practical feeling—the fact that, as content, it demands to be objective, but, as form, as a feeling, it is not—that serves as the motivating force that moves the will to begin to pursue definite ends, to begin the process of expression. The feeling for sociability, for instance, could compel an agent to seek such associations. However, Hegel is clear that a practical feeling is not sufficient unto itself to be motivating; it becomes so only to the extent that its contradictory status is found by the will to be in contradiction with its, that is, the will's, own nature. In other words, a practical feeling becomes a compelling source of action only insofar as the immediacy of its ought-character is taken *by the will* as something not simply from which it should withdraw itself, but as being an affect that obliges it to respond to its merely sensuous, particular, subject-bound condition. The will is disposed to respond to the discordant status of practical feeling by nothing less than its own nature for, as an affectivity, the normative force of practical feeling stands as a challenge to its fundamental self-relation, its determining of itself. The wellsprings of human action are thus, for Hegel, twofold: (1) the discord between the content and the form of practical feeling, and (2) its own drive to be what it is, namely self-determining, to realize its own universality, in and through the natural particularity of practical feeling. As Hegel puts this point: "The immediacy of feeling is, for the self-determination of the will, a negation; it therefore constitutes the will's subjectivity, which ought to be sublated [*welche aufgehoben werden soll*] so that the will becomes identical for itself" (*Enz. 1817*, §392).

An action, for Hegel, is thus initiated when the will takes up and incorporates a practical intuition, and it does so whenever it makes the fulfillment of such a feeling's normative content its end so that, through it, it actualizes itself as autonomous. When this occurs we have what Hegel labels drive (*Trieb*) and inclination (*Neigung*) and, insofar as such an end is pursued wholeheartedly, in a way that is unable to be deterred or diverted, that is, when the "totality of practical spirit places itself into a single one of the limited determinations [practical feelings]," we have what Hegel calls "passion [*Leidenschaft*]" (*Enz. 1817*, §392). All action, all expressivity is thus, at its core, on Hegel's theory, the manifestation of drive and inclination and, in its highest form, it is passionate.

Drives, inclinations, and passions differ from practical feelings in that they are all forms of striving, whereas practical feeling never rises above the level of passive receptivity. It is the difference between finding one's self with a sense that the world ought to be defined by equality and actually pursing this end. In the latter, the act arises out of a striving to integrate the normative content of a practical feeling into the will as an objective realization of its self-determination. Now insofar as this integration is successful, that is, insofar as the normative affectivity becomes a genuine expression of one's self-determination, the content of original moral intuition, which demands to be made truly and concretely universal and objective, is posited and pursued as an acknowledged end, as what Hegel terms an "interest [*Interesse*]": "nothing comes about," Hegel tells us, "without interest" (*Enz. 1817*, §394).

But with this transformation, the problem of the justificatory insufficiency of practical feeling reappears, albeit in a new, more complex form. The content of any interest pursued by the will remains something taken over from practical feeling. Subjective sense is now an end in the process of becoming objective and, accordingly, the normative content of the former is borne by the latter (see *Enz. 1817*, §395). But this incorporation of practical feeling into the will has only rendered it preliminarily motivational; it has not invested it with any justificatory authority. Drives, inclinations, and passions remain just as incapable of establishing the normative warrant of the various interests that they pursue as practical intuition had been. Hegel argues that without this warrant, there is no way to adjudicate among the interests that drives, inclinations, and passions pursue when they conflict with one another, as they inevitably do: the satisfaction of one may, in the most extreme case, necessitate the sacrifice of another, and without a pre-given, natural hierarchy, there is no way to tell which interest(s) are to be subordinated to others. As such, and to get at what is at stake here in its broadest terms, whenever one acts, the activity of willing itself stands under the threat of being torn between a multitude of different ends, all pulling in different, even opposed, directions, all claiming binding authority, but none possessing such. In this condition, the will's very autonomy itself is sacrificed for, as Hegel claims, if our drives, inclinations, and passions are indeed without warrant, then they are wholly particular and therefore "essentially infected by contingency, and related to the individual, as to one another, according to an external, unfree necessity" (*Enz. 1817*, §393).

Hegel's analysis of the motivational structure of action thus led him to identify a fundamental problem at the very core of willing itself: if one simply follows one's passions, genuinely autonomous willing—willing that is true to its own nature, its own universality—is inevitably lost in the morass of the conflicting, even irreconcilable, natural interests that it finds bearing down upon it. To express one's drives, one's inclinations, one's passions and to rely upon them alone is therefore ultimately self-defeating, since it denies the very concept of freedom upon which it is predicated. As wholly natural, the will is in contradiction with itself.

Hegel's decisive insight is to see that the root of this problem is essentially twofold: (a) the absence in the account thus far of any kind of reflection, that is, any kind of second-order appraisal or judgment as to the rightness or worthiness of any of these interests as ends to be pursued, and (b) the absence of any kind of criterion or measure by which interests as ends could be assessed and ranked (see *Enz. 1817*, §395; *GPR* §17). The two go hand in hand. Hegel shows that thought, in its highest form, is an "act of determining" (*Enz. 1817*, §386) and, as such, always works in accord with some principle(s). Thus far in the analysis, affectivity has set the agenda for action, and it has done so through its incorporation into the will's activity. But its ultimate effect has been to sever the will from its own essence. What is needed, if willing is to be genuinely expressive, is an assessment and ranking of interests, and this can only come by virtue of appeal to a principle that transcends the indeterminacy, the contingency, the particularity, of mere affectivity. In a word, it requires what Hegel will call a "measure [*Maß*]."

The Measure of Freedom: Happiness and Autonomy (*Enz. 1817*, §§395–99; *GPR* §§8–24)

We thus come back to our guiding question: What does it mean for the particular to be "reflected into itself," and how does this bring the will back to, that is, complete, its universality, its self-relatedness in individuality? Our examination of the will's particularity in the form of its moral psychology has shown that normative affectivity, on its own, suffers from what we have called justificatory insufficiency and that, as such, the will's particularity requires reflection and, with this, a criterion. The concern now is to see how these elements enter into the unfolding of the concept of willing without being extrinsic impositions upon it, that is, without violating the strictures of immanence, for it is only insofar as reflection and its standard are shown to be immanent to willing itself that we will have made a real advance in answering our question.

The account of reflection and its criterion differs between the *Encyclopedia* and the *Philosophy of Right*. In the *Encyclopedia*, Hegel moves directly from the problem of conflicting interests to the issue of the criterion, which he identifies as happiness (see *Enz. 1817*, §395), and he then draws out the consequences of this for the reflectivity of the will, namely that it is condemned to caprice and arbitrariness (see *Enz. 1817*, §§396–98). From this, he argues that only "the absolute individuality of the will, its pure freedom" (*Enz. 1817*, §399) can fulfill the role of the measure in such a way that the will is able to be truly autonomous. In the *Philosophy of Right*, however, Hegel's analysis develops from the issue of reflectivity directly and shows how this immanently leads to the more fundamental issue of the criterion and from this to the principles of happiness and freedom. Accordingly, as the latter is a more sustained and developed argument, we will follow its line of development.

Hegel proceeds, once again, from the discord between the form and the content of practical feeling. Drives, desires, and inclinations as moral sentiments incorporated into the will—what he here calls the "*immediate* or *natural* will" (*GPR* §11)—all strive after a normative content that is inherently universal and thus objective, but, as affectivities, they and their objects remain, in form, wholly particular and subjective. The content of such sensuous strivings is, Hegel says, "rational in itself; but expressed in this form of immediacy, it is not yet in the form of rationality" (*GPR* §11).

As such, drives and inclinations suffer from what Hegel here calls, expanding on his initial account of their conflictual nature, a "double indeterminacy" (*GPR* §12). Quantitatively, there is an unorganized and ill-defined "mass and multitude" of drives (*GPR* §12); while, qualitatively, each drive itself points to a variety of different ends and an equally diverse set of means by which they can be satisfied. We desire equality; we have a drive for sociability. Each can denote a quite different state of affairs; each can be realized in a number of different ways. In their immediacy, there is no rhyme or reason. All bear upon us with equal normative force.

Hegel argues that the will initiates a distinctly free act, that is, it begins to express itself, by taking up both sides of this indeterminacy and settling on a definite course of action, what he calls "resolving [*Beschließen*]" (*GPR* §12): the will selects one drive, one of that drive's ends, and one of its ways of being fulfilled to pursue. To resolve, then, we could say, though Hegel does not employ this terminology in the *Philosophy of Right*, is the volitional act that engenders what he had called an "interest" in the *Encyclopedia* account (see *Enz. 1817*, §394).

Hegel's claim is that resolution remains, at this stage, distinct from the content of drives, inclinations, and desires and that, as such, it can only be formal and thus wholly abstract (see *GPR* §13). The "resolving will" stands aloft, with itself in its universality, over and above both the quantitative and qualitative particularity of its sensuous drives, desires, and inclinations. Yet for it to act at all, it must take up a drive and strive after it. The will is, Hegel says, a "*choosing* [*wählen*] between these determinations, all of which in this respect are external to me" (*GPR* §14). In this sense, Hegel concludes, the will is choice (*Willkür*, *GPR* §15), but precisely as such, as choice, it is at once free and dependent, universal and particular; in short, it is a "contradiction" (*GPR* §15A).[16] Standing above any and all immediacy, in its own immediate self-relatedness, the will is free from any extrinsic determination, able to select its course of action; and yet, in order for it to be what it is, that is, for it to be willing, for it to act, it is essentially bound to the content of its drives and inclinations, for these are the means and motivational foundations of its own expressivity. Thus, if the will indeed does nothing without seeking to fulfill an interest upon which it has resolved, then in choosing to pursue any interest it finds itself immediately at odds with its very own nature. Resolution and choice are therefore the will in self-contradiction.

Hegel has thus shown that the conventional depiction of freedom, its "commonest representation" (*GPR* §15A), the ability to choose, is indeed an essential moment in the concept of the will. Expression is an act of choice. But, as essential as it is, being able to resolve on a course of action between a multitude of indeterminate desires and to choose to pursue some end as one's interest, Hegel contends, only exposes the extrinsic dependency of this view of the will. It can select any path that it wants as long as that path is rooted in a moral sentiment, for it is only from this wellspring that motivational force flows. Yet, as we noted in our discussion of the *Encyclopedia*'s account, motivational force does not entail justificatory standing. As a result, choice can be nothing more than arbitrariness. And this is precisely now the issue that Hegel raises in the *Philosophy of Right.*

The analysis thus far has established a fundamental correlation: the indeterminacy of drives, desires, and inclinations (*GPR* §§11–12) is matched by the indeterminacy of the will as choice (*GPR* §§12–15): "The contradiction, which is choice [*Willkür*, §15], has *appearance* as a *dialectic* of drives and inclinations, which conflict with each other in such a way that the satisfaction of one demands that the satisfaction of the other be subordinated or sacrificed, and so on" (*GPR* §17). But Hegel now identifies, in a way he had not in the *Encyclopedia*, what he clearly takes to be the common root of both forms of indeterminacy:

> Since a drive is merely the simple directionality of its own determinacy and therefore has no measure [*Maß*] within itself, this determination that it should be subordinated or sacrificed is the contingent decision of choice, which may be guided by calculative understanding as to which drive will afford the greater satisfaction or by any other consideration one cares to name. (*GPR* §17)

Hegel introduces here what will turn out to be the pivotal premise in his argument. Drives and inclinations, in and of themselves, have no measure, that is, they have no inherent principle by which they can be ordered with respect to one another; they thus have no mark immanent within them that would compel one (or one set of) drive(s) to be satisfied over against and before another. A desire for equality, for example, does not, of itself, dictate whether it should or should not take precedence over a desire for sociability. Each inclination indicates only a general course of action, a heading that can be undertaken, but it does not specify how this course should be related to any others. It is, thus, as a result of this lack of measure that the domain of moral affectivity, even after it is incorporated into the will through resolve and choice, that is, after it has become a set of interests, remains an unordered heap, quantitatively and qualitatively indeterminate. And it is due to this same lack that the will is condemned to being nothing more than mere caprice and arbitrariness.

A measure, then, is what is required to solve the problem of justificatory insufficiency. It does so by being at once a principle of judgment and a principle of action, that is, insofar as it brings together the question of justification and that of motivation.[17] A measure enables an agent to discriminate between the overwhelming variety of drives, desires, and inclinations and decide which ones ought to be subordinated to others and which are to be sacrificed for the sake of others. It thus provides a criterion by which the double indeterminacy of the particular can be fashioned into a coherent, even systematic, order.

As the principle that determines this hierarchical order, it is ultimately for the sake of the measure that an agent acts. Accordingly, such a standard is also what moves one, what authoritatively binds and compels an agent to undertake a course of action. Hegel has clearly shown that there is no act that does not rise out of the springs of affectivity. But he has also just as clearly shown that the account of the moral psychology of action cannot end there. For a desire to be motivating, it must not only be compelling in itself, it must be determined through reflection to be justified in the claim that it makes upon the will. Hence, when one acts in accord with a true measure, one is acting on a desire that one has resolved upon and chosen, but one is doing so only insofar as the normativity of that desire has been established by the measure.[18]

There are obviously two fundamental concerns here, and each goes to the very core of what a measure is and what it does. First, a measure could serve as a principle of judgment and a principle of action and could be imposed extrinsically upon an agent's practical feelings, desires, and interests, the domain of the will's particularity. The standard account of practical agency takes precisely such a view: action occurs when the law of reason imposes its constraint upon the morass of sensuous desires from on high. But clearly, on Hegel's terms, this would count as particularity reflected not into itself, but into another, not an integration of particularity and universality, but the subsumption of the former under the latter. The measure at issue must thus, in Hegel's account, be immanent within particularity itself.

Secondly, though immanent, the measure cannot be simply identical with normative affectivity. It cannot itself be a moral sentiment or feeling for, as Hegel makes clear in the passage cited above, no desire bears within itself a standard whereby all other desires can be assessed and ranked. Now, to be sure, Hegel's point here is not that the problem of justificatory insufficiency means that moral sentiment is devoid of any normative content. He continues to maintain that our moral senses are filled with concrete obligatory force, that they bear an irreducible ought-character.

So, to note that moral affectivity, precisely in its immediacy, lacks an inherent, pre-given order is thus not to reject moral sentiment out of hand. Rather, the lack of measure is a claim that goes to the *form* of such intuitions, not to their *content*. Insofar as they remain immediate, even after they are taken up and endorsed in resolution and choice, they remain indeterminate with respect to their relationships with one another, and it is this indeterminacy that renders both them and the will that seeks to pursue them contradictory.

The measure at issue here must thus meet four fundamental conditions: (a) it must be a principle of *judgment*, (b) it must be a principle of *action*, (c) it must be *immanent* within practical affectivity, but (d) it must *not* be simply another *affect itself*. But what standard can serve as such a criterion? What kind of a measure can genuinely be such a measure of freedom?

Surprisingly, Hegel's response to this central question begins from the claim that the work of reflection, as it looks to such a measure as this, is defined by the idea of "*purification* [*Reinigung*]." He argues that, due to the contradictory nature of drives, desires, and inclinations, they must be judged as good insofar as they are immanent determinations of the will, possessing genuinely normative content, but, in terms of their form, they must be judged as evil since they are "*determinations of nature*, opposed to freedom and to the concept of spirit in general" (*GPR* §18). As evil, they are to be "*eradicated* [*auszurotten*]," and from this it follows, he says, that there must be a general "*purification of the drives*" (*GPR* §19). Now, having invoked language that clearly suggests the elimination of drives and which thus appears to play into the standard dualistic model of the inherent conflict of reason and desire, Hegel quickly notes that what is to be eradicated or purified here is not desire as such, and certainly not its content, but purely its form: immediacy. "In the demand for the *purification of the drives* is the universal representation that they should be freed from the *form* of their immediate natural determinacy and from the subjectivity and contingency of their *content* and brought back to their substantial essence" (*GPR* §19). The task of reflection is thus to eliminate the mere immediacy of the will's drives and, in doing so, bring these affects to their own proper essence, that is, bring the subjectivity and particularity of their form into accord with the objectivity and universality of their content. To reflect is thus to purify, and Hegel's usage of the same term to describe this work here as he had employed to explain the definition of the individuality of the will in §7, *zurückgeführen* (to bring back or restore), clearly signals that this purifying process is central to his account of freedom. It is nothing less, we can say, than the reflection of particularity that brings it into accord with its content. But how exactly does this achieve the integration of the universality and particularity, the individuality, of the will?

In its initial attempt to purify the drives, reflection takes the concept of happiness (*Glückseligkeit*) as the criterion for estimating, ranking, and, where necessary, sacrificing desires. Hegel defines happiness as the maximal fulfillment of all compatible practical desires, what he calls the "whole of satisfaction" (*GPR* §20; see also, *Enz. 1817*, §396). Now, it is important to note that the satisfaction at issue here is not simply the fulfillment of any or all inclinations. As we noted above, Hegel had already restricted the discussion to the concept of practical feeling and its affective descendants, all of which are distinguished by possessing an inherent ought-structure. Happiness here is thus not about maximizing simple sensuous gratification; it is not about seeking mere pleasure, as the Platonic tradition, for instance, assumes. Rather, to pursue happiness, in this context, is to pursue the fulfillment of all of our *moral* intuitions insofar as they are or are able to be rendered consistent with one another. In this sense, happiness, as in the Aristotelian tradition, might be better captured by the notion of personal and interpersonal flourishing, that is, of leading a life that embodies what our moral sentiments, at bottom, most want.[19]

Hegel argues, however, that, though this eudaemonistic sense of happiness meets the conditions of being a principle of judgment (one can discriminate between various drives and inclinations as to whether they contribute, or not, to an overall goal of leading a truly satisfied life), a principle of action (a life of maximal fulfillment does appear to be a sufficient enough incentive to act), and of being immanent within affectivity (happiness is nothing more than a sum total of the fulfillment of practical drives), it remains, nonetheless, a "*formal universality*" (*GPR* §20). As a "whole of satisfaction," happiness is an idea that reflection generalizes via abstraction from what the variety of practical affectivity possesses in common. As such, its content is set not only by the normative content of practical feeling, drive, and passion, but by their form of immediacy as well. It is not only immanent with practical affectivity, it remains identical to it. As a result, happiness is necessarily infected with the contingency, indeterminacy, and subjectivity that define the form of this domain and, accordingly, it can purify practical desires only by seeking to harmonize them under this abstraction, in what Hegel refers to as a wholly "external manner" (*GPR* §20) or, as he puts this point in the *Encyclopedia*, with happiness "subjective feeling and whim must tip the scales [*den Ausschlag geben muß*]" (*Enz. 1817*, §396; see also, *Enz. 1817*, §398). Happiness thus fails to purify the form of immediacy that governs the will's particularity. Paradoxically, then, precisely by remaining identical to practical affectivity, and especially to its form, happiness is a reflection of the particularity of the will not into itself, but into another, into an abstraction, a generalized particularity, drawn from this very well that, as a result, fails to overcome its defining indeterminacy. How, then, is the will's particularity to be genuinely reflected into itself and thereby brought back to its universality?

Hegel's answer is that the requisite measure is not to be found in the formal universality of happiness, but in the concrete universality of freedom. The latter, Hegel says, is the "truth" (*GPR* §21) of the former. Now, our examination of the method of systematic justification in chapter 1 showed that the linear progression from one concept to another is actually, if carried out in accordance with the strictures of immanence and necessary entailment, a retrogression back into the ground of the prior concept, and that is exactly what claiming that freedom is the truth of happiness means here. Hegel contrasts happiness as a universal that is formed simply by generalizing abstraction from practical affect, and, as such, turns out to be an extrinsic measure, with freedom, as the will's own defining essence, which he calls here "*self-determining universality* [*die sich selbst bestimmende Allgemeinheit*]" (*GPR* §21). In taking freedom as its end, then, the will is seeking nothing less than itself: "its object is itself, and is therefore neither an *other* [*Anderes*] nor a *restriction* [*Schranke*]; instead, in its object it [the will] has returned to [*zurückgekehrt*] itself" (*GPR* §22). Freedom thus now wills freedom, and in having itself as its content, object, and end, that is, in being autonomous, Hegel says, "the will is free not only *in itself* but also *for itself*—the truthful idea" (*GPR* §21).

Now, while it might seem obvious to conclude that the proper measure of freedom is nothing other than freedom itself, the claim raises two absolutely fundamental questions: How does self-determination as the proper measure of genuinely free willing follow, immanently and necessarily, from happiness? And, furthermore, how does it satisfy the fourfold condition for being such a measure that we examined above?

Consider first the structure of the general argument that Hegel is making. Systematic justification's fundamental commitment, we recall, is to set aside all assumptions, to suspend all assumptions that might serve as preconceptions about the nature of the object it seeks to examine and, instead, to faithfully observe the way in which the matter at issue develops wholly of itself and thus how it itself demands to be thought. Philosophical science therefore seeks to do nothing other than attend to the immanent conceptual unfolding of its object and this means, as we saw, the development of one concept into another where laying out the essential properties or determinations of the former necessarily entails the latter. In the present context, the matter at issue is the will and, specifically, what constitutes free willing. Hegel has argued that, in any act, an agent is always compelled to act out of some practical feeling, where this feeling has been incorporated by the will and endorsed as its own, that is, as it is made its interest. But, even as so incorporated, interests lack any kind of inherent order of preference and compatibility. As a result, reflection is needed, and to do its work, it must seek out a standard to guide it in assessing which interest(s) the will is truly justified in pursuing. Happiness is the initial determination of such a measure, since it is nothing less than the fulfillment of the sum total of all normative affects. Now, as the totality of practical affectivity, it remains immanent to the motivational wellsprings of action, but, as merely what all such desires have in common, that is, as an abstract whole, it necessarily remains indeterminate and extrinsic, a vacuous generality whose content must inevitably be drawn from the subjective immediacy of desire itself. It is thus this inadequacy, its lack of immanent conceptual determination, that forces the concept of happiness beyond itself to the concept of freedom. But how does freedom solve the problem of extrinsic indeterminacy?[20]

The key lies in Hegel's claim that the concept of freedom is a "self-determining," rather than a "formal" kind of universality. As we have seen, a formal universality is simply the abstraction of what is common to a set of particulars that is, then, used to subsume those particulars under it as its instantiations. A self-determining universality, which Hegel also refers to as a concrete universality (see *GPR* §24A), on the other hand, is not a generalization; rather, it is a universality whose essence or identity comes into its own, comes to be what it is, in and through its immanent differentiation, that is, in its specifying of its own particularity wholly from within itself. Concrete universality, in this sense, can be said to determine itself, to be "self-determining," since it is only in and through this othering *of* itself *from within* itself that it is what it is. The concept thereby becomes idea. Hegel's argument is thus that the will is a self-determining universality precisely insofar as its particularities, its practical affections, are its own immanent differentiations. They are so only insofar as the will incorporates the normative intuition present in practical feeling as a resolved and chosen interest, thereby making it its motivation, and when this is done because the intuition in question enables the will to be with itself—that is, be its universality, its self-relatedness, in and through this particularity—its justification. Accordingly, the incorporation of feeling into the will through reflection and under the measure of self-determination purifies the feeling in question: it frees it from its natural immediacy and brings its form into accord with its normative content. The universality of the will, its pure self-relatedness, thus determines its own otherness, its particularity, and becomes itself, becomes acts of free, expressive willing, precisely in and through this self-othering. The self-determining universality of freedom therefore follows immanently and of necessity from the formal universality of happiness because freedom cancels the externality of happiness that resulted from its fateful identification with the particularity over which it sought to generalize, while taking up and preserving its immanence with the particular in the movement of its own self-differentiation. Hegel expresses this conclusion in what is surely one of his densest formulations:

> The will that *is in and for itself* has the will itself as such, thus itself in its pure universality, as its object—this universality is such that the *immediacy* of naturalness and the *particularity*, with which naturalness is likewise caught up, are both sublated [*aufgehoben*] within it [the will] when it [this universality] is produced by reflection. (*GPR* §21A)

The will is "*with itself* [*bei sich*]" (*GPR* §23) or at home with itself—that is, it is conscious of itself as its end, in control of itself, as a result, and comes to be what it is through particularizing itself in this way[21]—whenever it pursues its normative affects by reflecting upon them by means of the only standard that proves to be endemic to them: freedom as self-determination. To seek after freedom is thus nothing less than the process of the will's particularity, its normative affects, being reflected into itself and, by virtue of nothing other than this reflection, being brought back to its universality, its being-with-itself in and through the determination of its own otherness. As such, this process of willing is the will in its complete individuality.

The decisive element, then, in Hegel's systematic demonstration of freedom is the notion of individuality understood as autonomy, for it is this concept alone that proves to fulfill the fourfold condition of the measure of the will. Let us consider each requirement briefly again in turn. Autonomy serves as a principle of *judgment* insofar as it enables reflection to discriminate between drives, desires, and inclinations, identify those that can be taken up as interests and pursued as ends through which the will can be genuinely with itself, and rank them in order of which ones fulfill this function more fully and completely than others. Autonomy serves as a principle of *action* insofar as it is ultimately for its sake that the will acts in pursuing any and all of these distinctive kinds of purposes. And autonomy is a measure *immanent* in, but *not identical* to, practical affectivity, since it is what makes such sentiments genuine motives, and it is by virtue of this principle that the normative authority that they claim is established.

In beginning our examination of Hegel's account, we noted his claim that the deduction both "*that* the will is free and *what* the will and freedom are . . . takes place only within the interconnections of the whole" (*GPR* §4A). We have now seen, by following the strictures of systematic justification and the ontology that it entails, that willing must necessarily be conceived in terms of spirit and thus as the practical self-relational processes, the self-determinings, of a natural organism and why, as a distinctly free expressive process, this demands to be thought through the concept of individuality.[22] But because this raised the question of the roles of practical feeling, drive, and interest and, accordingly, of choice, reflection, and its measure, we were necessarily led to the core thesis of Hegel's theory: the concrete universality of freedom is the only possible measure of genuinely autonomous willing.

Accordingly, Hegel's theory of freedom holds, in sum, that in any action, an agent acts on a practical feeling. Agents are thereby compelled to take a desire for their subjective end and bring it about in the world, making this end their interest. The motivational wellspring of every action is, then, some interest. But the motivation for a distinctly *free* action is interest(s) that satisfy the conditions of autonomy. And these sorts of interest are those in which the agent is able to be aware of the end as its own, in control of itself in the accomplishment of the end, and where, by accomplishing the interest, the agent is fulfilled. It is in this sense, then, that every free action is done for the sake of the concept of freedom itself. A desire is able to be an interest that meets these conditions if and only if it is purified, that is, only if it is freed from the natural immediacy of its form and the subjectivity and contingency of its content, and is restored to its inherent position within the rational hierarchy of desires. To be free, then, is for the natural processes whereby organisms express and govern themselves to bear and realize ends only insofar as they are pursued on account of and as justified by the principle of freedom itself. And this, we can now say, is what it means for the particularity of the will, to return again to Hegel's dense formulation, to reflect itself into itself and thereby be brought back to its universality.

But with this, Hegel tells us, paradoxically, we have arrived only at what he calls "the *abstract* concept of the idea of the will" (*GPR* §27, emphasis added). The account thus far has set out the basic structure of genuinely free willing: the will's being with itself (*bei sich selbst*), finding itself actualized in and through its pursuit of its ends as they are transformed, through reflection and its criterion, freedom, from moral intuitions to desires, inclinations, and passions, and from these to defining interests. And yet, this remains formal because freedom is defined here solely in terms of self-relationality, self-determination. Autonomy alone is a necessary, but not a sufficient, condition of freedom. To be truly self-governing, the will's determinations must be objective as well. Self-determination requires objectivity, and this takes us to the deduction of right proper.

Chapter 3

✦

Right

As we saw in the previous chapter, Hegel's account of freedom holds that for an act to be genuinely free, it must meet two mutually necessary and sufficient conditions. It must express an end in such a way that the agent, by virtue of this act, is self-determining, and the act must result in the end becoming actual. What is required in order to satisfy the former condition—what we called the self-determination condition—was spelled out in terms of the ontological concept of the individuality of willing, and it placed the focus on issues of motivation and justification. The latter requirement—the objectivity condition—is concerned with matters of what can be called normative social ontology, and it places the deduction of right at center stage as freedom's actuality or idea.

According to that proof, the concept of right follows, immanently and necessarily, as the completion of the unfolding of the concept of freedom. Right, in this sense, is freedom's "*result*" (*GPR* §2). But, as we saw in our discussion of the method of systematic normative justification in chapter 1, such a linear progression must not be understood, as classical foundationalist models hold, as a derivation from a more basic, noninferential axiom; in the case at hand, the concept of freedom. Rather, right stands as the *result* of freedom precisely because right, and right alone, is the set of essential relations that constitute the concept of freedom itself. Conceptual progression, in systematic normative justification, is retrogression into the ground upon which the concept with which it began depends. Accordingly, the deduction of right, which, for these reasons, necessarily stands outside the science of right itself, establishes right as not only the result of freedom, but as its "truth" or *ground* as well (*GPR* §2).

Given this, the fundamental task of the science of right proper—and that is to say, though it is not often acknowledged as such, the fundamental task of moral, legal, social, and political philosophy for Hegel—proves to be nothing less than setting out what it means for right to be, at once, the result, truth, and ground of freedom. The science of right thus works from this distinctive determination of right as its systematic, nonrepresentational "*starting point*" (*GPR* §2) and seeks to observe its own immanent development. This science, then, is the unfolding of the concept of right, its immanent self-differentiation, into its own complete determination, its idea, or, as Hegel puts this in the declaration that opens the *Philosophy of Right*: "The *philosophical science of right* has the *idea of right*, the concept of right and its actualization, for its object" (*GPR* §1). But what precisely does it mean for right to be the result, truth, and ground of freedom? And what does Hegel mean by the idea of right? The aim of the present chapter is to answer these fundamental questions. To do so, we must begin, as we did in our examination of the concept of freedom, with the systematic concept under which Hegel treats this question: Objective Spirit. This will lead us into an investigation of the deduction of right and of its basic nature and this will, in turn, allow us to set out the master argument of the science of right itself.

Objective Spirit (*Enz. 1817*, §400; *GPR* §§3–4 and 25–29)

Objective Spirit is the concept under which Hegel elaborates the philosophical science of right in the *Encyclopedia*.[1] And though the concept is explicitly referred to only in a couple of minor passages in the *Elements of the Philosophy of Right* itself, it nonetheless marks a crucial distinction that provides an essential pathway into the concept of right and into the science that this text sets forth.

Now, as we noted in chapter 2, Objective Spirit is distinguished from Subjective Spirit in terms of their different relationships to the domain of nature. Subjective Spirit is an account of the various self-relational expressive movements of organisms that includes, at its pinnacle, the treatment of the will, agency, and freedom that we explored in chapter 2. Hegel tells us that all these forms are defined by their "finding [*vorfinden*]" the natural world as always already given, as their "presupposition" (*Enz. 1817*, §306 [§305]), and, in turn, their seeking to make this their own, a relationship that we traced in the case of the expressive activity of the will in relation to the natural affects: practical feeling, desire, and passion.

Objective Spirit, by contrast, does not simply presuppose nature. Rather, it is, Hegel tells us, an account of the "originating or setting up [*Erzeugen*] of spirit's own world as one posited [*gesetzen*] by it" (*Enz. 1817*, §306 [§305]). Hegel clearly appeals to this same concept in the following line from the *Elements of the Philosophy of Right*: "the system of right is the realm of actualized freedom, the world of spirit produced [*hervorgebracht*] from out of itself as a second nature" (*GPR* §4; see also, *Enz. 1817*, §400). Objective Spirit is thus a world (*Welt*), one set up or posited in the movement of manifestation that is the freedom of the will. But, as we have seen, the activity of the will is always set in motion by virtue of the world of nature—specifically, the domain of practical feeling—upon which it thus rests, and, in this sense, it is a second nature.[2] But what does it mean to claim that Objective Spirit is a world and a second nature that is the actualization of the will in its freedom and thereby serves as its ground?

It has been tempting, given these definitions—particularly with the invocation of the traditional notion of "second nature," affirmed from the Aristotelian tradition through Plutarch to Montaigne and beyond as the essence of custom or habit—to interpret Objective Spirit in sociological and descriptive terms, or what I think is best referred to as a culturalist framework. This interpretation, which can be traced back to Hegel's immediate contemporaries, has been most persuasively articulated and defended in our own time by Nicolai Hartmann who, we should note, clearly acknowledged his *departure* from Hegel's own systematic conception when he wrote in the early 1960s that

> the concept of Objective Spirit is *not* a consequence of the system or a product of the dialectical train of thought. In fact, *it is not a speculative doctrine at all, but a straightforward descriptive concept*, a philosophical formulation of a basic phenomenon that allows at any time of demonstration and description *independently of* the [philosophical] standpoint. In a word, it is an original intuition, a discovery on Hegel's part of something that stands on its own two feet.[3]

On this interpretation, Objective Spirit is an account of the conventions by which a society organizes and understands its uniquely shared existence; it is simply given, an "original intuition," and as such, stands in no need of further justification, and is a wholly *descriptive* and *sociological* concept.

This culturalist view still defines the parameters of more recent interpretations. The two principal variations in the current literature are the *linguistic model* and the *recognitional model*. The former conceives of Objective Spirit as the norms or rules embedded in the common meanings and shared (principally linguistic) practices by which the world that we inhabit together is rendered intelligible.[4] The latter defines Objective Spirit as the distinctly modern intersubjective conditions of mutuality that enable each of us to sense, interpret, and realize our needs and interests as fully autonomous beings.[5]

However, the problem with both of these models, for Hegel, is that they are fundamentally representationalist. Each takes social life, and its interrelations, for granted; they presuppose the irreducibly shared rules and conventions of society that transcend the agency of individuals. To be sure, they derive the distinctive features of this sociality as conditions of communication or genuine self-determination, but the determinate nature of such conditions is itself largely taken over from their historical pre-givenness. Institutions, on both these interpretations, are nothing more than the always already given layers that set down the horizons of sense within which mundane acts become meaningful. But insofar as these models take their object of inquiry over ready-made from (empirical) intuition, it follows that they render the justifications and claims they make about the norms and structures of sociality vulnerable to the skeptical challenges of the Agrippan trilemma. Objective Spirit, in these readings, is therefore either arbitrary, viciously circular, or opens upon an infinite regress. And as a result, these accounts render the principles, practices, and institutions of Objective Spirit as unwarranted restrictions (*Beschränkungen*) of freedom, rather than as its immanent result, truth, and ground, or what Hegel will simply call freedom's existence (*Dasein*).

As we examined in chapter 1, it was precisely these kinds of concerns about the ability of forms of knowledge rooted wholly in representation to establish normative warrant that led Hegel to propose a distinctly systematic form of moral, legal, social, and political philosophy. And the hallmark of this approach is, of course, its unrelenting commitment to complete presuppositionlessness. Methodologically, this means that a truly systematic justification of right must begin by disengaging from all that it might take for granted; in this case, the social world that we inhabit. The philosophical science of right therefore must seek to do nothing other than attend to the immanent conceptual unfolding of its object—*Recht*—for it is only in abiding by this primary stricture of radical immanence that dogmatism and skepticism can be avoided. But what does such a method as this mean for the concept of Objective Spirit? What would a truly immanent, nonrepresentational concept of Objective Spirit be?

To address these questions, it will be helpful, once again, to turn to the distinction between systematicity and representation. In the Remark to *GPR* §3, Hegel distinguishes the systematic concept of right from the empiricist (Romantic) conception of positive law or positive right. Positive right refers to the legal code and judicial system required by any actual state, and on the empiricist account, as we noted in chapter 1, the justification of its normative authority is provided by inquiry into whether its institutions and practices flow from the unique historical needs, circumstances, and traditions of the society over which it has been set in place.[6] As a systematic concept, Objective Spirit is thus not, as the Romantics held and as the contemporary culturalist interpretation and its variants now contend, the historically varying social rules and conventions that transcend the agency of individuals and within whose framework they operate.

Yet Hegel is equally clear that Objective Spirit is not to be equated with the rationalist (Enlightened Absolutist) view that positive law derives its authority from a wholly transcendent order of nature, natural right or natural law (*Naturrecht*).[7] In the Remark to *Enz. 1817*, §415, at the end of its account of property, contract, crime, and punishment—or what Hegel here calls simply Right, but would come to call Abstract Right—he contends that a profound "ambiguity" lies in the term *Naturrecht* itself: on the one hand, it may refer to right as "*something implanted,* as it were, *immediately* through nature," or, on the other hand, it may conceive of right as "determined by the nature of the matter, that is, by the *concept*."[8] The former sense, he notes, had been dominant in the modern tradition of political reflection and had given rise to the idea of a distinction between a state of nature, where the principles of natural right are supposed to govern, and civil or political society, where the prerogatives and duties prescribed by natural right must be restricted and freedom itself must be restrained or even sacrificed for the sake of security and survival. Objective Spirit is therefore not, as the Enlightened Absolutists contended, a pre-given providential natural order upon which the institutions and practices of political society must be grounded and their actuality assessed.

But if Objective Spirit is neither of these representationalist conceptions—neither historical rules and conventions nor the transcendent principles of a natural order—then what is its systematic concept?

Let us recall again the definitions with which we began. Objective Spirit is (1) the "originating or setting up [*Erzeugen*] of spirit's own world as one posited [*gesetzen*] by it" (*Enz. 1817*, §306 [§305]), and (2) "the system of right is the realm of actualized freedom, the world of spirit produced [*hervorgebraucht*] from out of itself as a second nature" (*GPR* §4; see also, *Enz. 1817*, §400). Objective Spirit is a world set in place by freedom, a world rooted in the domain of practical feeling, and therefore a second nature. But how is this precisely not then a sphere of custom and tradition?[9]

On the systematic account, Objective Spirit is, necessarily and at once, normative and ontological. We can best see this by examining Hegel's deduction of the concept of right and its employment of the notion of the objectivity of freedom: "The absolute determination or, if one prefers, the absolute drive, of the free spirit (§21) is for its freedom to be its object [*Gegenstand*]" (*GPR* §27). As we saw in chapter 2, Hegel's account of the self-determination condition demonstrates that for any act to be free requires that the reflection guiding it must take freedom itself as its ultimate motivating criterion. Picking up this thread, Hegel argues that what follows from this is that for the will to be genuinely free, genuinely self-determining, it must take freedom itself as its highest good, as its ultimate end: "In having universality, itself as infinite form, as its content, object, and end [*Inhalte, Gegenstande und Zweck*], the will is free not only in itself, but also for itself—the Idea in its truth" (*GPR* §21). The immanent unfolding of the concept of freedom thus shows not only that freedom is the true essence of willing, but that willing comes to be itself only insofar as it pursues its interests by taking freedom as its ultimate object, that is, as the highest good in view of which it ranks and assesses all other goods.

At *GPR* §27, Hegel returns to this idea of freedom being the proper object of the will and argues, pivotally, that being such an object (*Gegenstand*)—that is, being the highest good, the ultimate object of free acts—entails that freedom must not only be a criterion, but it must also be objective (*objectiv*) and this in two distinct, though related, senses: "in the sense that it [the free spirit] is to be the rational system of the spirit itself, and in the sense that this system is to be immediate actuality (§26)" (*GPR* §27). This twofold sense of the objectivity of freedom, I contend, defines, for Hegel, the systematic as opposed to the representational concept of Objective Spirit. But what precisely does this twofold sense mean?

Note that Hegel refers us here back to *GPR* §26, where he tells us that the will can be said to be *objektiv* in three senses. The first is where the will accords with its own concept, that is, with self-determination, and is thus most truly itself. The second is where the will is immersed in its object and is not in relation to itself. And the third is where the will fulfills its ends in external existence, but in accordance with the principle of self-determination. In defining Objective Spirit as a world and this world as a second nature, Hegel is appealing to the first and third of these senses of "objective," which I shall call the normative and the ontological respectively, and his claim is that they are necessarily mutually implicative: to be what it most properly is, freedom must be actual; for freedom to be actual, it must be in accord with its concept, which is to say, freedom must not only be a principle of action, but normative and ontological as well.[10]

Let us consider each of these senses in more detail. The normative sense has to do with the nature of universality. As we saw in chapter 2, when judged in terms of the principle of self-determination, the range of practical affects—feelings, desires, passions, or interests—can be purified of their subjective immediacy, ranked with respect to one another, and raised to the universality of form that their content, their ought character, had always demanded. Hegel now argues that the universal standing of these principles, that they are authoritative for everyone and at all times, flows not only from their being specified by the concrete measure of freedom, that is, by its form of self-relation, but from their actually being posited by this kind of willing itself. That is to say, freedom becomes objective when the motivational wellsprings from which the will acts, its particularities, are actually promulgated by itself as universally valid. Freedom in this initial sense of objectivity is thus constituted in and through the will's reflective purifying and positing of its own determinations as the objective principles with which it is itself, in turn, obligated to comply. It is in this sense that the will can be said to fully accord with its own concept.

The objectivity of freedom refers in the first instance, then, not, as the representationalist cultural model holds, to a set of habits or customs or even to the rules or conventions of a shared life, but to the collection of universally binding norms that constitute the will's fundamental duties, or what Hegel calls the "rational system of the will's determinations" (*GPR* §19; see also, *GPR* §27). Hegel's point is that the rightfulness or normativity of such principles, their authoritativeness, is something with which they are endowed by virtue of their being essential elements that define genuinely free willing. It is thus the will's distinctly autonomous positing that sets the mark for what is right. Consequently, freedom can be said to be objective in this first sense as a result of the will's unique activity of taking up its own particularity, purifying it of its immediacy, and, from it, creating and setting in place the system of norms to which it is then bound. Objectivity as normative universality therefore originates in the unique self-legislating activity of the will or, as Hegel puts it, the activity of the will consists in "sublating [*aufzuheben*] the contradiction between subjectivity and objectivity and in translating [*übersetzen*] its ends from their subjective determination into an objective one, while at the same time remaining *with itself* [*bei sich*] in this objectivity" (*GPR* §28; see also, *GPR* §22).

Turning now to the ontological meaning of the objectivity of freedom, Hegel argues that for the rational system of norms that the will engenders through its self-legislative activity to be truly universal, truly authoritative, truly right, it must be concretely actual as well. The objectivity of freedom cannot simply be a matter of universal validity, for this would leave the object of the will's positing, namely right itself, as a set of unrealized norms standing over against the immediacy of the external world. In this sense, the will would not be truly existent. As such, the form of the norms that it sets down would still be in discord with their content. Consequently, for freedom to be truly objective, it must be embodied in determinate and concrete existence, or what Hegel in the passage above refers to as "immediate actuality," and this means that the universal validity of right must be institutional as well.[11] Freedom is objective in this sense, then, only insofar as it is, we could say, housed in resilient structures whose normative and symbolic content and associated practices define and sustain a rightful, and a just, social order.[12]

Hence, to say that Objective Spirit is a world and a second nature, systematically, is to say that it is a set of interdependent normative institutions and practices that embody and thus house, in making possible and in supporting, the freedom of Subjective Spirit; it is a set of actually existent norms that are binding because they are the essential determinations of the will's freedom incorporating its natural motivating affects, its first nature, in accordance with the concrete universality of the principle of freedom. Accordingly, Hegel concludes the deduction of right with the following famous definition: "*Right* is any existence [*Dasein*] in general that is the *existence* of the *free will*.—Right is therefore in general freedom, as idea" (*GPR* §29). We showed in chapter 1 that as the conclusion to the systematic justification of right, this definition must be read, fundamentally, in two ways. First, right is the result (*Resultat*) of freedom. It is that concept to which the immanent unfolding of the concept of freedom—its becoming concrete—necessarily leads. Accordingly, right is the embodiment of what it is to will, what it is to be free; it is the actuality of the concept of freedom, freedom as idea. But this deduction also establishes that right is not just the result of freedom, but is its ground (*Grund*) as well. Right, then, is what enables the will to be free. Willing is what it truly is, namely autonomous, if and only if it is embodied in some objectively existent "thing": some determinate kind of end, duty, or institution. Right, in this sense, is the otherness in and through which willing is able to express its interests, control itself in doing so, and thus be genuinely self-determining. All of which is to say that right is the "retrogressive ground" of freedom. It is, at once, the result that is necessarily and immanently entailed by the conceptual unfolding of freedom—and, in this sense, the nature of freedom that we explored in chapter 2 determines the precise nature of the content of Objective Spirit—but right is also the set of norms, practices, and institutions that make self-determination itself possible. Objective Spirit, then, is the objectivity of freedom, its very existence, rather than its restriction. It is the rational system of norms that constitutes the will's essential ends and these ends only as they are concretely actualized in a social-political world comprised of institutions specified wholly by them.

Now, it is important to note that, with this account of the concept of Objective Spirit and the deduction of right, we have only reached the beginning of the science of right proper. Hegel is clear that the systematic concept of right is but its "determinate *starting point* [*Anfangspunkt*]" (*GPR* §2). The task of the science is "to observe the immanent development of the matter itself" (*GPR* §2). That is to say, the subject of the science of right—notwithstanding what one may gather from the current literature—is not freedom, or practical agency, or the justification of right, or even recognition. Rather, it is the vigilant commitment to set aside all presuppositions and unfold the determinations of the concept of right precisely and only as these determinations flow immanently and necessarily from the concrete nature of the concept itself. Now, an analysis of these determinations is, of course, beyond the purview of the present study, but it will be useful to complete our examination of right by considering the basic structure of Hegel's account. To do so requires exploring two of its most crucial features: (1) the science's fundamental organizing principle, which I propose to call the Axiom of the Hierarchy of Right, and then (2) its core line of argument, the Master Argument of the Science of Right.

The Axiom of the Hierarchy of Right (*GPR* §30)

Right is, as we have seen, both the result and the ground of freedom, and Hegel refers to this at *GPR* §30 in a rather startling, and little commented upon, way: right, he says "is, above all, something *sacred* [*Heiliges*] solely because it is the existence of the absolute concept, self-conscious freedom" (*GPR* §30). Now, by this odd turn of phrase, Hegel is not saying that right is divine (*Göttliches*); rather, he is marking, at once, its unique status—that, as the existence of freedom, and thus as genuinely authoritative, right stands apart from everything else that simply exists—and its wholeness in the sense of being complete, self-sufficient.[13] But this declaration raises an important question. As it stands, the sacredness of right seems to be nothing more than a name for its vacuousness, its emptiness, for, as simply the existence of freedom, it appears to lack any definition, any concreteness. Accordingly, where does the determinacy of right, its definition, come from? Put slightly differently, how are the essential specifications that comprise right and are thus the proper object of the science at hand here to be spelled out?

Hegel acknowledges this issue—designating it the "formalism of right"—and responds by laying down the axiom that will govern the very structure of the science of right itself:

> The *formalism* of right, however, . . . arises out of the differences in the development of the concept of freedom. By contrast with the more formal, that is, *more abstract*, and hence more restricted kind of right, the sphere and stage of spirit, in which spirit has determined and actualized within itself the further moments contained in its Idea, has, as *more concrete*, a higher right, for it is richer within itself and more truly universal. (*GPR* §30)

The determinations of right flow directly from its being the result and ground of freedom and, precisely as such, they form a hierarchy. The determinations of right that are the more complete embodiment of freedom—that is, the ones that are more concrete, richer, more universal—have a higher normative standing (they are the "higher right") than the ones that embody freedom to a lesser degree.

In one sense, of course, this axiom is simply an instance of the general principle, which we explored in chapter 1, that the result of a systematic demonstration is the ground of the concept from which it is derived. But more is actually being said here, and it is significant because, as we shall see, it serves to organize the entire account of right.

So what does it mean for something to count as a more complete actualization of freedom and thus to be a higher kind of right? A more complete embodiment of freedom is, first, one that fulfills more of the particularity of the will, more of the practical feelings, drives, desires, inclinations, and interests that make up its motivating grounds; and, second, it is one that fulfills them in a way that is more concrete, that is, more stable and assured, more securely sanctioned. To put the point another way, the forms of right that enable willing to be more fully and completely self-determining, to be with itself in and through their otherness, are of higher rank, are more authoritative, than those that serve this end to a lesser extent. In terms that we have just explored, the institutions of right have a higher normative status than the universal scope of its basic principles because the institutions and practices of right constitute a more complete and determinate space in and through which agents are able to express themselves in a fully autonomous fashion.

To illustrate Hegel's claim with the divisions of the science of right to which we shall return in a moment, the axiom entails that Abstract Right, which is concerned primarily with the ownership of property, is a lesser form of right, that is, it is less binding, because it embodies the universality of the will, than the more concrete universality of the particularity of the will, well-being and happiness, that is the concern of Morality.[14] And higher than either of these domains stands Ethicality because it fulfills these interests in the more concrete, more stable, and thus more fully self-determining institutions of the family, civil society, and the state. Accordingly, Ethicality is a domain of right that is higher, more right, more just, more binding, than either Abstract Right or Morality. And it is precisely this hierarchy—that the institutions of right are higher than its sheer principles precisely because the institutions embody these principles—that dictates the structure of the science as a whole.

Hegel notes that without the hierarchy it sets in place, that is, if all domains of right stood as equally normative, then they could come into irresolvable conflict with one another, and this would require that one kind of right be restricted by or subordinated to another, rather than integrated and fulfilled by one another. "Morality, ethicality, the interest of the state—each is a distinctive right because each of these shapes [*Gestalten*][15] is a determination and existence of *freedom*. They can only come into *collision* insofar as they are all on the same footing in that all are rights" (*GPR* §30A). The problem of a collision or conflict between domains of right is only possible, then, insofar as they are not integrated into a proper hierarchy; that is, as Hegel puts it here, insofar as "they are all on the same footing." Now, what the Master Argument of the Science of Right, which we will examine shortly, purports to demonstrate is precisely the proper hierarchical integration of the domains of right so that they are not all on an equal footing. But if we assume for a moment that they are all the same, what kind of collisions might occur?

An important conflict between the domains of right that Hegel himself treats in the main body of the science revolves around the "right of necessity [*Ius necessitatis*, *Notrecht*]" (*GPR* §127). This right, which had its roots in the moral theology of the twelfth century was taken up in the natural rights and social contract theories of the seventeenth and eighteenth centuries and is treated in some depth by both Kant and Fichte, asserted that human beings may take whatever measures are necessary to save their lives in situations of extreme need or necessity (*Not*). The canonical example of such a situation was that of two shipwreck survivors clinging to a plank (later, a lifeboat) that is unable to sustain them both, and it asked whether either of them has the right to sacrifice the life of the other. Hegel takes up the question in a significantly different variation: in a condition where one's very existence is threatened due to a social, rather than a natural, cause, does one have the right to take the property of another, where that property is needed for his survival, without proper transfer of its title, for example, stealing a loaf of bread in a condition of extreme deprivation?[16]

On Hegel's account, such a right poses a conflict between the rights of ownership established under Abstract Right and the right to well-being justified by the principles of Morality. Put simply, it is a question of whether there can ever be a legitimate right to steal. Hegel's contention is that if both of the forms of right in question are equal, that is, if they are equally binding, then there would be no way to adjudicate the conflict because in the absence of a criterion establishing their proper relationship, their proper rank, one right has as much validity as the other. Now, as we noted, the argument set forth in the science of right, following the Axiom of the Hierarchy of Right, purports to show that Ethicality is the higher domain of right that integrates these lower spheres and resolves such conflicts by establishing institutions that ensure that both the right to property ownership as well as the right to well-being are not only promulgated, but enforced as well.[17] What, then, is this argument, which I have proposed to call the Master Argument of the Science of Right, that establishes the higher authority of Ethicality with respect to Abstract Right and Morality?

The Master Argument of the Science of Right (*Enz. 1817*, §429; *GPR* §141)

There is a fairly conventional way of portraying the main line of argument of Hegel's science of right: the norms of Abstract Right and Morality, that is, of property ownership and moral conscience, prove, on closer inspection, to be wholly and irrevocably vacuous and, as such, to be incapable of serving as principles to guide conduct or the development of character. Therefore, in a kind of reductio ad absurdum, such normative guidance can only come from the concrete ethics, the Ethicality, that one's historically specific social role(s)—as family member, as producer/consumer, as citizen—can provide.[18] Now, while this outline is not completely without merit, it is, of course, clearly premised on what we have seen is a fundamentally representationalist interpretation of right, one that equates *Sittlichkeit* (which we have translated as Ethicality, but which more often has been rendered as "ethical life") with its ordinary nineteenth-century German sense, "customary social morality," and *Sitte*, from which it derives, with custom, habit, and mores. Hegel is making, as we have seen, a strictly systematic argument and, following the Deduction of Right and the Axiom of the Hierarchy of Right, to demonstrate that one domain has a higher normative standing than another requires showing that it embodies freedom more completely and more concretely. So the question must be: How is the core argument of the science of right an instance of systematic normative justification?

Following the Deduction of Right and the Axiom of the Hierarchy of Right and in accordance with the strictures of systematic normative justification, to demonstrate that *Sittlichkeit* (Ethicality) has a higher normative standing than either Abstract Right or Morality requires showing that (1) *Sittlichkeit* is entailed immanently and necessarily by the unfolding of the concept of right as the objectivity of freedom, and that (2) *Sittlichkeit* embodies freedom more completely and more concretely than do the domains of Abstract Right and Morality.

The argument proceeds in three stages. The *first stage* shows how the basic concept of right, precisely as the objectivity of freedom, necessarily develops into the domains of Abstract Right and Morality. The *second stage* then demonstrates that these domains necessarily reach their own immanent contradiction in the relationship between conscience and the good. Finally, in the *third stage*, the relationship of conscience and the good is shown to be necessarily plagued by abstract indeterminacy, and this very indeterminacy is then shown to entail the integration of Abstract Right and Morality in the domain of *Sittlichkeit*.

*Stage I: Abstract Right and Morality (*GPR *§§34–127;* Enz. 1817, *§§402–21)*

Abstract Right sets forth the minimal principles—those of what Hegel calls Personhood—that are necessary for free willing to be possible: to be free requires being able to own things as property and this is, ultimately, to be able to transfer title to (to alienate) that object via different kinds of contractual relations. However, the possibility of entering into such intersubjective agreements necessarily exposes ownership to the vagaries of individual choice (*Willkür*) and thus to caprice, for example, to the failure of contractual partners to fulfill their obligations, and thus specifically to various types of wrongs: non-malicious wrong, fraud, and crime.

Abstract Right is an enforceable right in that wrongs committed against it are acts of coercion against the most rudimentary form of the existence of freedom. As such, these acts merit proportionate punishment. Yet to mete out such sanctions requires evaluating the acts in question as acts of choice (which Hegel here calls the free will "for itself" as distinct from Abstract Right's account of the free will "in itself"; see also, *GPR* §104), and that necessarily means in terms of the motivations (the purposes and intentions) that compelled them. But precisely this requirement takes the concept of right beyond its initial determination as Abstract Right, the existence of freedom's universality, to its more concrete determination as Morality, the existence of the will's particularity, and to what Hegel terms the domain of Morality.

Morality lays down the basic principles of willing as particular, concrete, and determinate—the norms of what Hegel calls Subjectivity. To be a subject is, fundamentally, to strive to bring about one's aims. But Hegel shows that in seeking after a purpose, one necessarily seeks a broader set of aims than the specific goal of the action—for example, the satisfaction of desires, happiness, well-being—that is to say, as Hegel puts it, one always necessarily *intends* more than one *purpose*: satisfying one's own desires is necessarily, at the same time and ultimately, motivated by seeking the desires, the well-being of others, or what Hegel terms simply the totality of one's own and all others' ends, life itself.

*Stage II: Conscience and the Good (*GPR *§§128–40;* Enz. 1817, *§§422–28)*

Hegel contends that the preceding analyses of Abstract Right and Morality show, on the one hand, that the *universality* of Personhood (Abstract Right) immanently and necessarily entails, via the requirements of punishment, the *particularity* of Subjectivity (Morality) (see *GPR* §106), and, on the other hand, that the *particularity* of Subjectivity (Morality) immanently and necessarily entails, in the encompassing totality that is the ultimate good of life, the *universality* of Personhood (Abstract Right). As such, the first two determinations of right—its universality and its particularity—thus stand in a necessary relation to one another. This relation takes the form of the good, that is, the totality of vital needs, life, the "*fulfilled* universal, determined in and for itself," and of conscience, where subjectivity is the ultimate arbiter of what is good, that "infinite and inwardly knowing subjectivity that determines its content within itself" (see *GPR* §128). The relation is, as Hegel notes, relative, which is to say, the relation is contingent and the relata separable, insofar as it expresses an obligation that ought to be fulfilled, but that may not be: the good (the universality of right) ought to be realized in conscience (the particularity of right) and conscience ought to embody what is truly good.

As noted above, it is precisely to illustrate the relative nature of the claims of Abstract Right and Morality that Hegel, in this context, appeals to the "right of necessity [*Ius necessitatis*, *Notrecht*]" (*GPR* §127). As an entitlement to take what is needed regardless of title when one is in a condition of extreme deprivation, it exposes the contingency of the relationship between the normative standing of the ownership of property and the needs of life.

Accordingly, as each requires the other to be what it is, but each equally is unable to be integrated with the other, both the good and conscience, and that is just both Abstract Right and Morality, stand empty of any determinate criterion and thus any valid content, that is, any obligations or duties (see *GPR* §§135, 138; and *Enz. 1817*, §§422–27). Observing the immanent unfolding of the concept of right thus shows that, precisely as the objectivity of freedom, right immanently and necessarily entails its own other: not only in the form of the possibility of wrong (*GPR* §§82–103; *Enz. 1817*, §§409–414), but ultimately as the very possibility of giving precedence in action to particularity over universality, that is, to the possibility of evil itself (*GPR* §§139–40; *Enz. 1817*, §§427–28). Abstract Right and Morality thus reach, in this possibility, a contradiction: each requires the other, but neither is able to be integrated or fulfilled in the other.

Stage III: The Integration of Abstract Right and Morality in Sittlichkeit *(*GPR *§141;* Enz. 1817*, §429)*

The third and crucial step of the argument takes up this moment and demonstrates that it entails the domain of *Sittlichkeit* (Ethicality). The case for this claim is set out most fully at *GPR* §141. Accordingly, it is necessary to examine the line of argument developed in this passage rather carefully.

Hegel begins by summarizing the conceptual situation with regard to the problem of the universality and the particularity of right, and he formulates it precisely in terms of the problem of the relative relation of the good and conscience that we just reviewed in Stage II.

> For the *good*, as the substantial universal of freedom, but as something still *abstract*, determinations of some kind and the principle for determining them (although this principle is identical with the good itself) are *required*; likewise, for *conscience*, the purely abstract principle of determination, it is required that its determinations should be universal and objective. Both of them [i.e., the good and the conscience], each raised to be totalities for themselves, become the determinateless [*Bestimmungslosen*] that *ought* [*soll*] to be determined. (*GPR* §141)

Now, in what is surely the key move of the overarching train of argument of the science of right, Hegel infers from this mutual lack of determinacy of the good and conscience that their integration as moments of a unity that is more fundamental than either is already accomplished, albeit only implicitly, insofar as the sheer vacuousness of each renders them identical to one another:[19] "But the integration of both of these relative totalities into absolute identity is already accomplished *in itself* in that this very subjectivity of *pure self-certainty*, melting away for itself in its vanity [*Eitelkeit*], is *identical* with the *abstract universality* of the good." The basic insight driving this admittedly strange inference—an outlandish move from ought to is—is the notion that without any determinacy, conscience and the good cannot be held distinct from one another and are thus necessarily identical. The evidence for this to which Hegel appeals here is the claim that without a criterion to justify its conduct, conscience, the particularity of right, is necessarily free to indulge its every whim, making its behavior a condition that Hegel refers to as vanity, and this is just what the good, the criterion required by conscience, the universality of right, is, the endorsement of any and all whims, precisely insofar as it too is abstract. But rather than taking this insight as a sheer *reductio*, Hegel argues that the identity that these two moments together constitute is actually a totality that is itself distinct from the relative relationship of conscience and the good because, as the integration of the one in the other, the whole they form is concrete, which is to say determinate. As a result, and following the Axiom of the Hierarchy of Right, this totality is more fundamental, a higher, more authoritative form of right than either conscience (Morality) or the good (Abstract Right), and it is properly that from which both necessarily derive their own normative validity.[20] This whole is *Sittlichkeit*: "the identity—which is accordingly *concrete*—of the good and the subjective will, the truth of them both, is *ethicality* [*Sittlichkeit*]." The Remark to *GPR* §141 lays out the basic organizing structure of this argument. Its key point is that the fundamental identity that conscience and the good form is set out explicitly, that is, as Hegel puts it, it is posited, just insofar as they "sublate themselves [*sich aufheben*]." By this, he means that, as indeterminate, the good and conscience negate their own independence, that is, their separability, their finitude, their limitedness, and, precisely as equally indeterminate, they also thereby reveal their dependence on one another to be what each is. It is thus the self-sublation of each moment that shows them to be moments of a greater unity, a unity that becomes manifest only in and through the revelation of the reciprocal interdependence of these moments. In this way, *Sittlichkeit* is therefore proved to be the integrating unity that is, at once, the *result* and the *ground* of Abstract Right and Morality.

Hegel's claim is that this identity is the basis for a systematic, rather than representationalist (what we have also called a culturalist) conception of

Sittlichkeit, and this concept serves as the highest determination of right and thus as the proper culmination of the argument that the science of right seeks to make. The concreteness of *Sittlichkeit*, as a systematic concept, lies, then, not in its being a historically specific set of expectations embodied in the customs, conventions, and patterns of life of some definite society. One's duties are not, in fact, prescribed by one's historically contingent station. Rather, the concrete identity of conscience and the good, of the particularity and universality of right, denotes the institutional order (the ethical objectivity) that the complete actualization of freedom as self-determination demands—the ethical institutions, as Hegel shows, of the family, civil society, and the state—and the dispositions (the ethical subjectivity) required to live in accordance with the norms embodied in this order. Though the precise features and justifications of these institutions are beyond the scope of the present study, we can see from this overview of the master argument that where the objectivity of freedom sets the standard for the determination of what these institutions must be, what their internal structures are, and what their relationships with one another must comprise, there the potential conflicts between the principles of Abstract Right and Morality are resolved and the ethical objectivity of *Sittlichkeit* is able to be the rightful criterion to which ethical subjectivity—to live a life that exhibits true conscience, virtue, and rectitude—is obligated to measure up. It is in this sense, then, that Hegel is able to conclude that *Sittlichkeit* is the highest determination of Objective Spirit, as both a world and a second nature, because it is the domain where the universal validity of the principles of Abstract Right and Morality is embodied in determinate, interdependent, existent, and normative social and political institutions. And *Sittlichkeit* is ultimately just what it means for right to be the "idea of right," the result, truth, and ground of freedom:

> *Sittlichkeit* is the *idea of freedom* as the living good that has its knowing, willing, and, through its acting, its actuality, in self-consciousness just as these have their foundation existing in and for itself and their motivating end in ethical being—*the concept of freedom become the present world* and *the nature of self-consciousness*. (*GPR* §142)

Conclusion

✦

Hegel's Critical Theory

The preceding pages have proposed an interpretation and defense of the systematic foundations of Hegel's philosophical science of right. They have sought to do so in a way that, unlike the main interpretative paradigms, is able to demonstrate the essential role that the systematic form and attendant metaphysical doctrines of his broader philosophical project play in addressing the problem of normativity generally, and thus their significance for the substantive normative claims of this particular science. To this end, we placed the distinction between representation and systematicity at the very center of the proposed readings of this science's method of justification, its conception of practical agency, and its underlying social ontology. The basic insight we derived is that genuinely normative claims, that is, ones that are buttressed against the classic challenges of skepticism, can only be established by a systematic form of argumentation, that is, by a type of justification defined by its radical commitment to refrain from any and all presuppositions, and by the metaphysics of freedom and right that this commitment necessarily entails. This is what marks the distinctive historical and contemporary contribution of Hegel's thought to normative philosophy and it is what entitles it, for Hegel, to be called a genuinely philosophical science. My conviction is that it is only once this groundwork has been laid that the core theses and doctrines of the science itself—that is, its accounts of property, ownership, contract, punishment, the principles of moral conduct, responsibility, and judgment, and the necessary social and political institutions and practices of a genuinely rational society—can even begin to be properly taken up, explicated, and their cogency assessed. Laying out these foundations has thus been the fundamental task to which this study has been devoted.

But even if this work has made some progress in meeting this rather lofty ambition, a vexing problem still remains. Our concern has been with the foundations of normativity: right as the result, truth, and ground of freedom. Yet such foundations are thought to be important not only in themselves, but for the way in which they provide standards by which existing social and political institutions, practices, and states of affairs, ones claiming to be genuinely authoritative, just, good, and right, can be examined and the soundness of their claims evaluated. In short, normative foundations make social and political critique possible. But, famously, Hegel is thought to mark the eclipse of precisely this kind of project. Philosophy is, he tells us, nothing but "*its own time grasped in thoughts*" (*GW* 14:1, 15), and we would search the entire expanse of his philosophical system in vain, it would seem, for a space for the classical evaluative function of reason. Is there any sense, then, in which we can speak of Hegel's own critical theory?

I want to conclude this study by arguing that the distinctive form of normative argumentation and ontology that we have sought to set out and explore in the science of right lays the basis for an equally distinctive form of normative critique, one where the distinction between systematicity and representation, which has been so central to the reading proposed in the present study, plays again a pivotal, though, as we shall now see, a decidedly different role. To set out exactly what is at stake here, let us begin by briefly expanding upon the challenge to such a project.

Is, Ought, and Accommodationism

In 1821, the year in which *Elements of the Philosophy of Right* was officially published—it was actually available by October 1820[1]—three reviews of the work appeared. The most extensive came from Heinrich Paulus, the rationalist theologian and professor of exegesis and church history at the University of Heidelberg with whom Hegel shared a rather long and somewhat complicated history.[2] Paulus identified a tension in the work between its conception of the task of philosophy—namely, as Hegel famously puts it in the "Preface," "to grasp [*begriefen*] *what is*" (*GW* 14:1, 15), a task founded infamously on the principle that "what is *rational* is *actual*; and what is *actual* is *rational*" (*GW* 14:1, 14)—and the text's repeated pronouncements about what exactly being rational demands of various social and political institutions and practices; a tension, in short, between is and ought.[3] And it was this tension that largely circumscribed the debates in the ensuing years regarding the nature of Hegel's personal politics, the politics entailed by his thought, and the science of right itself.

It proved extremely tempting to see Hegel's thought as just the ultimate expression of a much broader paradigm shift in German intellectual culture that took place during this time. The trajectory of German thought from the late eighteenth to the early nineteenth century has often been said to be a tale of the emergence and ultimate decline of the critical power of reason.[4] The era begins, in this account, with the Enlightenment struggle to establish reason as the supreme measure of truth, the final court of appeal, whose self-evident, universal, and impartial principles were to provide the foundations upon which natural science, morality, religion, and politics were to be justified and the standards against which all beliefs were to be judged. It was to be, as Kant famously put it, the "genuine age of criticism." But by the late 1790s a profound transformation in the purpose and meaning of reason was already afoot. Understanding how the institutions, traditions, and beliefs of a society arose from within a specific set of historical circumstances and setting out the laws that govern those developments came to replace the critique of social and intellectual commitments in terms of the timeless norms of rationality. At the root of this shift lay the metacritique of reason propounded by Hamann and Herder and the pervasive historicism to which this led, with its dogma that principles of reason are ultimately nothing more than expressions of the practices and conventions of historically and geographically unique societies. In a span of less than fifty years, the age of criticism had given way to the age of explanation.

Hegel's declaration that philosophy is "its own time grasped in thoughts" thus seemed to do nothing more than confirm this trajectory. Reason as the final arbiter of theory and of practice, it appeared, was to be cast aside in favor of a kind of resignation in the present and a recognition of the impotence of rationality. As a result, charges of accommodationism, conservatism, quietism, and even historicism against Hegel's political philosophy triumphed,[5] a conclusion that Ernst Tugendhat encapsulated in our own time in a famously damning judgment: "Hegel's philosophy is consciously and explicitly the philosophy of the justification of the existing order, quite irrespective of how this existing order may be constituted."[6]

The conventional response to these accusations among scholars of Hegel's thought has been primarily historical and biographical. The extensive similarities between Hegel's account of the state and the liberal reforms of the Prussian government first proposed by Heinrich Karl vom Stein, and later by Karl August von Hardenberg, as well as his personal support of reformist movements and organizations throughout his career, have been noted and cataloged.[7] But as important and necessary as this corrective has been, it nonetheless fundamentally fails to grapple with the deeper question: Does Hegel's mature thought enable, even require, a critical role for reason, a foundation upon which it can set forth a political agenda and critique the social institutions and practices of its day? That is to say, the standard response fails to lay down the philosophical underpinnings for any kind of theory of what Kant would have called the distinctly public use of reason in Hegel's thought.[8] Without this framework in place, scholars can certainly show that Hegel himself endorsed and even employed such a usage, but, in pursuing this issue in this way, they fail to demonstrate that his philosophy, in fact, warrants such a function for reason.

The Systematic and Extra-Systematic Functions of Reason

In order to show that there is, in fact, a theory, albeit admittedly incipient, of public reason in Hegel's work and that the space created by this account provides the basis for his unique critical theory, we must begin by recognizing a crucial distinction between what I propose to call the systematic and extra-systematic functions of reason in Hegel's thought.[9]

The distinction between the systematic and extra-systematic functions of reason refers to the roles that reason plays as it explicitly accomplishes tasks *within* the systematic presentation of the principles of knowledge and the largely assumed role that it plays *outside* the enterprise of systematic construction proper. Before going any further, though, it should be noted that the distinction proposed here is wholly heuristic in nature. Its usefulness lies solely in enabling us to isolate an operative conception of public reason in Hegel and in seeing, by comparison, the ways in which this conception converges and diverges from the explicitly thematized systematic function that has been the focus of the present study.

Let us begin, then, with a brief outline of the systematic function. Hegel identifies the principal task of reason with the pursuit of philosophical reflection. The aim of this distinctive form of thought, as we have seen, is to grasp the nature of what truly is in terms of the determinations of thought, the structures whereby being is what it is. Now, according to what Hegel himself calls the "indeterminate, preliminary, historical" sketch of the nature of philosophy that he provides in the "Introduction" and "Preliminary Conception" of the *Encyclopedia of the Philosophical Sciences in Outline*, this means to know things as they are in themselves, and this is to know them as they are constituted in and by the categorial structures of thought: "Philosophy is here taken to be the science of reason and, of course, reason insofar as it becomes conscious of itself as all being [*die Vernunft ihrer selbst als alles Seyns bewußt wird*]" (*Enz. 1817*, §5). The aim of philosophy, in this sense, is to know the truth of being.

But, if this truth is nothing other than the determinations of thought, then the science of reason must be an organization of these determinations such that their order captures the very structure of being, its joints and junctures, itself. The principle of such an organization of knowledge whereby the division and interdependence of the categories of thought are genuinely philosophical rather than merely arbitrary is the necessary development of thought, or what Hegel calls "the necessity of the concept" (*Enz. 1817*, §6). Accordingly, the distinctly philosophical enterprise is the construction of a systematic presentation of the fundamental principles of knowledge where the veracity of this knowledge is guaranteed not by its correspondence to some external state of affairs, but by the immanent arrangement and unfolding of this knowledge itself (see *Enz. 1817*, §7). To philosophize, then, is to grasp what is in its truth, and this is to set out the work of thought itself as a systematic totality. Philosophy, in this sense, is always, at once, knowledge of being and knowledge of thought, thought thinking itself and in so doing grasping the nature of that which it produces, being. It is the construction of a system that fulfills the demand of traditional metaphysics to know things as they truly are, but which does so by holding fast to the revolution wrought by critical philosophy, namely, the insight that the determinations of being must be traced back to their root in the spontaneity of thought itself (see *Enz. 1817*, §§18–14 (19), 27–28). That is to say, the task of philosophy is to know truth as nothing other than the movement of the concept.

Now, with this sketch of the systematic function of reason in hand, I want to turn to what might be best termed its extra-systematic function. By this, I mean the polemical employments of reasoning that are to be found in the prefaces and introductions of the main works of Hegel's corpus, but that are also evident in the occasional essays, speeches, and reviews that he authored throughout his life. The injunction with which he begins the "Preface" to the *Phenomenology of Spirit* (1807), a caution he repeats, albeit in varying terms, in all the prefaces and introductions of the major writings, can serve for us as a point of entry into this distinctive form of reasoning:

> In a preface it is customary to explain the goal that the author has set for himself, the circumstances of his writing, and the way he thinks the work relates to other, earlier or contemporary efforts at treating the same object. But in the case of a philosophical work, this custom seems not only superfluous but, in view of the nature of the matter at issue [*der Natur der Sache*], even inappropriate and contrary to its purpose. For whatever might appropriately be said about philosophy

> in a preface—perhaps a historical account of the work's standpoint and tendency, its general content and results, a string of assertions and assurances made here and there about what is true—none of this can be accepted as the valid way of presenting philosophical truth. (*GW* 9, 9)

Hegel's admonition here that the customary rules of presentation that govern the writing of prefaces and other preparatory pieces betray the mode of reasoning that is proper to the matter itself serves to distinguish the largely polemical argumentation that characterizes these writings from that of the scientific method of demonstration that is at work in the main body of the treatises that they introduce. Prefaces and introductions, then, can play no part in establishing the authoritativeness of the philosophical claims for which they prepare us. In this sense, one might say that these texts make use of a form of reasoning that stands outside the principles of genuine philosophical method and, as such, would appear to be wholly dispensable, superfluous.

And yet, Hegel ascribes a quite specific function to such texts: *Bildung*. He writes, again in the "Preface" to the *Phenomenology* and speaking of what it is to accomplish: "The beginning of formation [*Bildung*], of working one's way out of the immediacy of substantial life, must always first consist in acquiring knowledge of universal principles and standpoints, and working up to the thought of the matter in general [*dem Gedanken der Sache überhaupt*]" (*GW* 9, 11). The purpose of the extra-systematic texts, then, is to provide for this acquisition of universal principles and historical standpoints so that a rudimentary basis for grasping and judging the matter at issue is set in place before the properly philosophical work of abiding with the matter itself and its immanent unfolding can begin. In this sense, these texts cannot simply engage in sophistical rhetoric, seeking merely to persuade their audience of the usefulness of the system that follows. Rather, they must compel their readers to work themselves out of the immediacy of life's demands to the thought of what truly is. These writings and the form of reasoning that they embody might, then, more properly be classified as preparations for the work of systematic comprehension. The distinctive function of this extra-systematic form of reasoning is, therefore, social, cultural, spiritual, and intellectual formation. But how precisely does this type of reasoning actually perform this work? In particular, how does it motivate us *to* the truth *from* the truth?

These questions can best be addressed in terms of two aspects: (1) the *resource* upon which this form of rationality consistently draws, and (2) the *standard of judgment* to which it necessarily appeals, and addressing these questions will bring us back again to the distinction between systematicity and representation.

Consider first, then, the question of the resource. The extra-systematic form of reason draws its readers out of the mundane by appealing precisely to the concrete possibilities presented by the historical epoch in which it is written. In the prefaces to the *Phenomenology*, the *Science of Logic*, and the first edition of the *Encyclopedia*, this is marked by Hegel's repeated references to the "new era," the "time of birth," the dawning of a "new world," and the attainment of a "higher standpoint." On the one hand, these references to the present as a time of ripening clearly indicate the historical preconditions of systematic philosophy: that the construction of a genuine science of reason came to be possible only in the wake of the intellectual and political upheavals that transformed European society in the late eighteenth and early nineteenth centuries. But, on the other hand, they also serve as the motivational wellspring upon which reason draws to make the case for the standpoint of systematic philosophical reflection itself. Such reasoning takes the form of proclaiming that what the social and political events that define the new era have made possible, what they have vouchsafed for its inheritors, is both a blessing and a burden that must now be taken up and worked through in thought itself. On this view, then, the historical epoch has already disposed us for the work of science. To form ourselves out of our immediacy and into such a task thus summons us precisely from the unique state of affairs, the auspicious moment, we could say, in which we find ourselves. Hegel's claim is that the onus to make good on this actual possibility is therefore what serves to compel the readers of these texts into this new philosophical enterprise and also, as we shall see, into concrete social and political action.

Now, it is precisely in this latter respect that the distinction between representation and systematicity proves vital. To appeal to the present as an age ripe with possibility is necessarily to appeal to and thus to communicate through the employment of publicly recognized symbols and images that couch the present in narratival terms. This context then enables certain elements of the life-world of its audience to be seen as significant, and, as a result, they can be drawn upon to compel readers to emerge from the simple mundane immediacy of this world to take up the possibility that lies uniquely before them: the project of the systematic unfolding of the matter at issue itself, ultimately, the truth of being. But to appeal both to a narratival structure and to the distinctive elements of the life-world on which such a structure sheds light is to draw upon a set of historically specific social and cultural background conditions whose validities are taken for granted in this usage. As such, the extra-systematic employment of reason necessarily traffics in the domain of representation in order to lead its audience precisely into systematic philosophy.

Yet, does not the investigation that we have undertaken in this study teach us that, if the systematic is, in this way, irretrievably entangled with the representational, then it would thereby be exposed to all the threats of the Agrippan trilemma: arbitrary grounding, infinite regress, and vicious circularity? Which is to say, would not the extra-systematic form of reasoning condemn the systematic philosophy that it introduces to being nothing more than emotivism, historicism, in a word, sheer dogmatism?

Hegel is, as we have shown, clearly aware of this problem, and as a result, he does not approach the relationship of the extra-systematic and the systematic naively. The appeal to the present historical context must always be justified, he contends, by a criterion that is not itself simply historical. Rather, it must be a standard established wholly within and by the system itself. The systematic must dictate the usage of the representational. But by what standard? How are the set of circumstances that rightly dispose us toward systematic philosophy to be picked out from the blooming, buzzing confusion of historical detail?

The answer, though it remains largely implicit in Hegel's remarks, is nonetheless exceedingly clear. The distinction between systematicity and representation does not collapse. Rather, the criterion for the extra-systematic function of reason is necessarily the same as that for its systematic employment: truth conceived as the movement of the concept, and in terms of right or normativity, as we have shown, is nothing other than the objectivity of freedom. That the present age bears within it concrete possibilities of thinking and acting upon this principle is what enables these conditions, as opposed to others, to be singled out as the signs of the dawning of a new world. In this way, the system itself establishes the standard that defines the extra-systematic employment of reason, its public usage, and the principle by which it operates. The preparatory representationalist pathway into the system is thus governed by the very concept of truth and right that is established by that system.

The extra-systematic form of reason that we find in the prefaces, introductions, and occasional essays of Hegel's published writings can therefore be said to exhibit a distinctive form of reasoning whereby, as Kant famously puts it, one speaks as a scholar (*Gelehrter*) before the public. And such a function advances for Kant, and I will now argue for Hegel as well, a clearly reformist, rather than revolutionary or conservative, approach to social, cultural, and political change. Public reason is to act as a germ of intellectual freedom that promotes the slow, gradual development of ever greater civil freedoms.

"The Rose in the Cross of the Present"

The "Preface" to *Elements of the Philosophy of Right* is the best example of the extra-systematic, public usage of reason in Hegel's work. He concludes it with a by now familiar warning for his readers that "as a foreword, it in any case can only speak externally and subjectively about the standpoint of the writing it precedes" (*GW* 14:1, 17). Which is to say, as we have seen above, the "Preface" speaks polemically, rather than systematically. But, as we have sought to explore, speaking polemically, speaking representationally, for Hegel, is not simply to be dismissed out of hand. When it is properly rooted in the truth as established in the system itself, it can be an engagement in and with the public domain, in and with representation, an engagement that seeks precisely to shape public opinion in accordance with the normative principles, concepts, and institutions that only the system itself can justify.

The "Preface" begins by acknowledging the occasion for the book's publication, namely as a textbook outline of the basic concepts involved in the science of right, the subject upon which Hegel was lecturing, and thus as an aid for those who would be attending these courses. He also here acknowledges the work's distinctive form: a compendium of right with remarks designed to clarify the science's more abstract contents. This leads Hegel to a famous discussion, one we noted at the beginning of the present study, regarding the way in which a *philosophical* outline must differ from what counted even then as an ordinary textbook: its unique logical or systematic method in which "the content is essentially inseparable from the *form*" (*GW* 14:1, 6). Hegel then immediately applies this claim about the distinctive methodology of philosophy to the subject matter of the work itself:

> After all, the *truth* about *right*, *ethicality*, and the *state* is *as old* as *its exposition and promulgation in public laws and in public morality and religion*. What more does this truth require—inasmuch as the thinking spirit is not content to possess it in this proximate way—than that it be *comprehended conceptually* [*begreifen*] as well, so that the content that is already rational in itself wins a rational form thereby appearing justified to free thinking, which does not stop at what is *given* . . . but starts out from itself and thereby demands to know itself as united in its innermost being with the truth? (*GW* 14:1, 7)

Hegel expands upon this point, as is proper to a preface, in an infamous polemical excursus in which he rails against all those who would take right as simply given, that is, as being whatever is posited by the authority of the state (positivism), or that which all or most people endorse (coherentism), or even whatever is validated by the inner voice of feelings, the heart, or spirit (subjectivism).[10] But this leaves open the decisive question: What does it mean to comprehend right conceptually (*begreifen*) such that it is justified to genuinely free thinking?

Hegel returns to this issue only in the "Preface's" closing pages. There—in the context of the famous dictum that "what is rational is actual; and what is actual is rational"—Hegel defines the very task of philosophy itself as "comprehending conceptually [*begreifen*] *what is*" because "*what is*, is reason" (*GW* 14:1, 15). Consequently, philosophy is, as we have noted for Hegel, "*its own time grasped in thoughts* [*ihre Zeit in Gedanken erfaßt*]" (*GW* 14:1, 15).

Hegel explains that the actuality invoked here must not be equated with the merely existent, or with what is simply ephemeral, for the rational is to be recognized as "the substance that is immanent and the eternal that is present" precisely in "the semblance of the temporal and transient" (*GW* 14:1, 14). But it is Hegel's explanation of what it means to comprehend conceptually what is and to grasp one's own time in thoughts that takes us to the core of his extra-systematic usage of reason in this text:

> To recognize reason as the rose in the cross of the present, and to delight therein—this rational insight is the *reconciliation* with actuality that philosophy grants to those who have received the inner summons *to comprehend conceptually* [*begreifen*], and in this, what is substantial, to preserve their subjective freedom, and, at the same time, to stand with their subjective freedom not in something particular and contingent, but in that which is in and for itself. (*GW* 14:1, 15–16)

The key to this crucial passage lies, obviously, in its stunning and intentionally ambiguous imagery, that is, precisely in its representationalist appeal. The rose in the cross of the present is a metaphor that alludes, at once, to the symbolism of the seventeenth-century secret religious society, the Rosicrucians, who used a St. Andrew's cross and four roses as its emblem, and to Luther's coat of arms, which had a black cross in the midst of a heart surrounded by white roses. It clearly articulates Hegel's core claim that to comprehend the actuality of right conceptually is to recognize that underlying the contingencies of the present—which are sometimes horrific in their extremes (the painful cross of the present)—is a substantiality that is rational in itself (the rose of reason), and the task of philosophical science is, by laying out the systematic unfolding of right, to reconcile the rationality of the thinking subject with this rationality of the actual. Doing this achieves for this deep, perhaps often buried, truth of right a rational form, a systematic justification, and this produces the reconciliation of the demand of free thought to stand solely in that which is rational about right "in and for itself."

But as significant as this thesis is, even more significant, in this context, is the fact that its means of conveyance is precisely not through systematic proof, but through representation. I will leave speculation about any possible esoteric significance of the rose to others[11] and note simply that Hegel's usage of it is indicative of what we have called the extra-systematic mode of communication that is to be found in the prefaces. The image seeks to provide an avenue via representation by which its audience of Germanic Europeans, their life-world decisively shaped and molded by Lutheranism and the Magisterial Reformation more broadly, can raise themselves into the matter at hand and its unfolding in the main systematic text itself, namely the concept of right and its determinations, and it does so precisely by appealing to the "distinctive principle of Protestantism" and, more specifically, to the religious and intellectual upheaval that began, for Hegel, with Luther:[12]

> What Luther inaugurated as faith in feeling and in the testimony of the spirit is the same thing that the spirit, at a more mature stage of its development, endeavors to grasp in the *concept* so as to free itself in the present and thus find itself therein. (*GW* 14:1, 16)

Hegel's reading of this principle is that the subjective freedom that Luther inaugurated requires that only those beliefs that can be justified by thought are to be held as valid and that the proper standard for such justification is freedom itself, the ability of the one making the judgment to find herself, to be in relationship to herself, precisely in and through the state of affairs being assessed. Hegel here grasps his own time in thoughts, and he does so by seeing the present in which he is writing as necessary relative to its antecedent conditions, the contingent historical events that had decisively shaped the tradition in which he and his readers stand, in this case, the legacy of the Magisterial Reformation. Hegel takes the present state of affairs to be an actualization of, and thus grounded in, that concrete possibility and he seeks, by taking up this specific condition, to intervene decisively in its historical legacy.

Reason in its public usage here appeals to the vocation, the destiny, that is the possibility left by this form of Reformation, and it employs this possibility—rhetorically, even polemically now—as the motivational wellspring from which the call "to comprehend and present the state as an inherently rational entity" is issued. The "Preface," in this sense, implores its readers to make good on the claim that has been laid on them by the heritage upon which the present contingent state of affairs in which they live depends.

The core thesis of Hegel's critical theory thus holds that the world must stand judged before the principle of freedom, and it is on this basis that the public use of reason is able to set forth specific proposals for reforming the concrete social and political life-world in which it finds itself. Again, Hegel's reference to Luther is decisive here. For what the Magisterial Reformation began was a revolutionary turn to subjectivity, in the form of feeling and the witness of the spirit, and these, in turn, sanctioned the demands of conscience and the authority of conviction. And yet this inaugural moment, as decisive as it was and still is, remains, Hegel contends, incomplete. As the image clearly indicates, Hegel holds this movement to be only a turn inwards, towards inner faith, subjective feeling, and the intimacies of the believer's heart, a turn to subjectivity that stands at odds with the very message of substantial or objective freedom, of being with one's self in and through otherness, that the science of right itself establishes.

Hegel's critical theory thus proclaims—as Johann Arndt's old pietist Lutheran saying goes—a reformation of doctrine (*Lehre*) that calls out to be completed by a reformation of deed, of life itself (*Leben*).[13] The public use of reason here not only implores its readers to be faithful to their inheritance, but to build, to reform, to even transform this legacy. The historical move to subjective freedom must be completed by an equally historic move to genuinely objective freedom, and this means nothing less than publicly urging for the creation of concrete institutions of such freedom—family, civil society, and a constitutional monarchical form of government, in a word, the institutions and practices of right as these are set forth in the systematic account of *Sittlichkeit*—and criticizing historical conditions in which these institutions are missing or inadequately developed. This is what it means, then, to evaluate existing social and political institutions, practices, and states of affairs that profess to be authoritative, just, good, and right, by the principles and strictures set forth in the system's account of Objective Spirit. And it is in this way that the normative foundations we have examined make a genuine and distinctive form of social and political critique possible.

The social and political agenda that the public use of reason Hegel advocates always stands under the admonition that whatever it proposes, whatever transformation of life it is able to effect, these will always be open to the possibility of becoming other than they are. Just as the past lays out an array of concrete possibilities that can be taken up in the present, so the present necessarily remains fragile, contingent, groundless. The arrival of the rational order is not guaranteed, nor is its construction ever secure. The public exercise of reason is thus, for Hegel, an unending vigilance to grasp the movement of the concept in actuality so that the institutions that seek to embody it, remain faithful to it.

We can see then that Hegel's philosophy—embodied in the couplet: "what is rational is actual; what is actual is rational"—does indeed lay down distinctly systematic foundations for the justification of the public use of reason both to sustain the principles of rationality that have historically already come to shape the world in which it operates, and to propose specific reforms of that heritage that seek to make good on the promises borne within it. Hegel's thought thus provides a distinctive foundation for seeing the grasping of what is as the use of intellectual freedom—to think freely—that works to bring about civil freedoms and an institutional order that enables its citizenry to act freely. In so doing, it makes clear that the efficacy of genuine critique is never simply about the demands of timeless principles, but always the ways in which these principles enable appeals to the traditions in which one lives. Hegel's critical theory is, we might thus say, though he surely would not, a form of hermeneutic critique.

NOTES

Introduction

1. "Social ontology," in what follows, refers exclusively to Hegel's account of the ontology of the social, his theory, more precisely, of Objective Spirit, rather than any claims about the role that sociality might play in matters of ontology more broadly.

2. For a useful review of this issue, see Hans-Friedrich Fulda, "Zum Theorietypus der Hegelschen Rechtsphilosophie," in *Hegels Philosophie des Rechts: Die Theorie der Rechtsformen*, ed. Dieter Henrich and Rolf-Peter Horstmann (Stuttgart: Klett-Cotta, 1982), 393–427; and for an excellent overview and more recent assessment of the broader terms of the debate, see Jean-François Kervégan, *L'Effectif et le rationnel: Hegel et l'esprit objectif* (Paris: Vrin, 2007), 7–15.

3. Vittorio Hösle has forcefully argued that Hegel's project constitutes nothing less than a complete rejection of the very task of a normative theory; see his *Hegels System: Der Idealismus der Subjektivität und das Problem der Intersubjektivität* (Hamburg: Felix Meiner, 1988), 417–23. The present study stands as a response to this declaration.

4. On the contentious interpretive legacy of the work, see Manfred Riedel, ed., *Materialien zu Hegels Rechtsphilosophie*, vol. 1 (Frankfurt am Main: Suhrkamp, 1975); and Henning Ottmann, *Individuum und Gemeinschaft bei Hegel, Band I: Hegel im Spiegel der Interpretationen* (Berlin: Walter de Gruyter, 1977).

5. Major representatives of the systematic-metaphysical tendency include Hugh Reyburn, *Hegel's Ethical Theory* (Oxford: Clarendon, 1967); Manfred Riedel, *Studien zu Hegels Rechtsphilosophie* (Frankfurt am Main: Suhrkamp, 1969); Emil Angehrn, *Freiheit und System bei Hegel* (Berlin: Walter de Gruyter, 1977); Dieter Henrich, "Vernunft in Verwirklichung," in Georg Friedrich Wilhelm Hegel, *Philosophie des Rechts: Die Vorlesung von 1819/20 in einer Nachschrift*, ed. Dieter Henrich (Frankfurt am Main: Suhrkamp, 1982), 9–39; and Adriaan T. Peperzak, *Modern Freedom: Hegel's Legal, Moral, and Political Philosophy* (Dordrecht: Kluwer Academic, 2001).

6. Excellent statements of what has come to be called the non-metaphysical reading of Hegel can be found in its originator, Klaus Hartmann, "Ideen zu einem neuen systematischen Verständnis der Hegelschen Rechtsphilosophie," *Perspektiven der Philosophie* 2 (1976): 167–200; in the early work of his student, Terry Pinkard, "Freedom and Social Categories," *Philosophy and Phenomenological Research* 47 (1986): 209–32; and, more recently and in importantly divergent forms, in the work of Richard Dien Winfield, *Reason and Justice* (Albany: State University of New York Press, 1988); and Robert Pippin, *Hegel's Practical Philosophy: Rational Agency as Ethical Life* (Cambridge: Cambridge University Press, 2008).

7. Influential versions of this now somewhat neglected view can be found in Joachim Ritter, *Metaphysik und Politik: Studien zu Aristoteles und Hegel*

(Frankfurt am Main: Suhrkamp, 1969); and Charles Taylor, *Hegel and Modern Society* (Cambridge: Cambridge University Press, 1979).

8. The most prominent and substantive representative of the nonsystematic-nonmetaphysical view is Allen W. Wood, *Hegel's Ethical Thought* (Cambridge: Cambridge University Press, 1990).

However, there have been and continue to be important variants of this approach. Some scholars favor replacing the systematic and metaphysical foundations of Hegel's political philosophy with a version of the phenomenological approach found in Hegel's Jena period: see, for instance, Karl-Heinz Ilting, "Rechtsphilosophie als Phänomenologie des Bewusstseins der Freiheit," in *Hegels Philosophie des Rechts: Die Theorie der Rechtsformen*, ed. Dieter Henrich and Rolf-Peter Horstmann (Stuttgart: Klett-Cotta, 1982), 225–54; and Mark Tunick, "Hegel's Nonfoundationalism: A Phenomenological Account of the Structure of the *Philosophy of Right*," *History of Philosophy Quarterly* 11 (1994): 317–37.

Others have argued for a more broadly social scientific reading: Michael O. Hardimon, *Hegel's Social Philosophy: The Project of Reconciliation* (Cambridge: Cambridge University Press, 1994); and Frederick Neuhouser, *Foundations of Hegel's Social Theory: Actualizing Freedom* (Cambridge, Mass.: Harvard University Press, 2000).

9. The systematic-metaphysical interpretation of Hegel's science of right that I shall argue for in what follows thus goes beyond the claim that a systematic reading of Hegel's mature works requires that they be interpreted in relation to his wider speculative system because this is Hegel's own stated self-understanding; for this view, see Thom Brooks, *Hegel's Political Philosophy: A Systematic Reading of the Philosophy of Right* (Edinburgh: Edinburgh University Press, 2007), esp. chap. 1.

That this is indeed Hegel's own stated self-understanding is undeniably the case. My claim is that, beyond this important historical point, the very normativity of the concepts, propositions, and doctrines that the science of right sets forth can be justified against the classical challenges of skepticism only insofar as they are shown to be grounded in the distinctive method and metaphysics of Hegel's broader system. The systematic-metaphysical interpretation propounded here is thus a matter not only of historical accuracy, but of meta-ethical validity and soundness.

10. For an excellent account of the philosophical motivations underlying the history of system formation, see Angelica Nuzzo, *System* (Bielefeld: Transcript Verlag, 2003).

11. The centrality of presuppositionlessness to Hegel's philosophical project has been most forcefully articulated and defended by Stephen Houlgate, *The Opening of Hegel's Logic: From Being to Infinity* (West Lafayette, Ind.: Purdue University Press, 2006), chap. 2.

12. On the decisive role of skepticism, and the "Agrippan trilemma" in particular, in German idealism, see Paul W. Franks, *All or Nothing: Systematicity, Transcendental Arguments, and Skepticism in German Idealism* (Cambridge, Mass.: Harvard University Press, 2005).

Chapter 1

1. Though the account of Hegel's method of systematic normative justification in what follows diverges sharply from the orientation he proposes, the exploration

of these issues owes a profound debt to the pioneering work of Robert Berman in this field. See his "Categorial Justification: Normative Argumentation in Hegel's Practical Philosophy," Ph.D. dissertation, New School Graduate Faculty, August 1982.

2. For this characterization of the distinction between rationalist and empiricist conceptions of rationality, see Frederick C. Beiser, "Two Concepts of Reason in German Idealism," in *Internationales Jahrbuch des Deutschen Idealismus (2003) / International Yearbook of German Idealism (2003): Konzepte der Rationalität / Concepts of Rationality* (Berlin: Walter de Gruyter, 2002), 13–27.

3. On the theory and policies of Enlightened Absolutism in Germany, see Karl Otmar Freiherr von Aretin, ed., *Der Aufgeklärte Absolutismus* (Cologne: Kiepenheuer and Witsch, 1974); Leonard Krieger, *An Essay on the Theory of Enlightened Despotism* (Chicago: University of Chicago Press, 1975); and Franklin Kopitzsch, ed., *Aufklärung, Absolutismus und Bürgertum in Deutschland* (Munich: Nymphenburger Verlagshandlung, 1976).

4. On the development of Conservatism in Germany, see Klaus Epstein, *The Genesis of German Conservatism* (Princeton, N.J.: Princeton University Press, 1966).

5. For discussions of the political philosophy of German Romanticism, see Jakob Baxa, *Einführung in die romantische Staatswissenschaft* (Jena: Fischer, 1923); Jacques Droz, *Le Romantisme allemand et l'état* (Paris: Payot, 1966); Theodore Ziolkowski, *German Romanticism and Its Institutions* (Princeton, N.J.: Princeton University Press, 1990), chap. 3; and Frederick C. Beiser, *Enlightenment, Revolution, & Romanticism: The Genesis of Modern German Political Thought, 1790–1800* (Cambridge, Mass.: Harvard University Press, 1992), part 2.

6. Hegel, in this passage, has in mind, of course, Wolff's metaphysics, but the point applies to the broader rationalist tradition.

7. Hegel does not explicitly address the theories of the Conservatives. He instead analyzes the methodological weaknesses that they share with their empiricist brethren among the Romantics.

8. For a careful examination of the various interpretive proposals regarding the project of the *Phenomenology* with respect to the system, see Ardis B. Collins, *Hegel's Phenomenology: The Dialectical Justification of Philosophy's First Principles* (Montreal: McGill-Queen's University Press, 2013), chaps. 2, 11, 18, and 19.

9. My claim here is simply that insofar as the Science of Logic sets forth and establishes the method by which the rest of the system argues, its account plays a controlling role in all the subsequent analyses. In support of this approach, I appeal to Hegel's articulation of the relationship between Logic, Nature, and Spirit at *Enz. 1817*, §477 where Logic, in the properly philosophical way of construing the syllogistic structure of the system, is said to play the role of the originating middle term between the extremes of Spirit and Nature.

On the vexed problem of the exact relationship between the Science of Logic and the *Philosophy of Right*, see Herbert Schnädelbach, "Zum Verhältnis von Logik und Gesellschaftstheorie bei Hegel," in *Aktualität und Folgen der Philosophie Hegels*, ed. Oskar Negt (Frankfurt am Main: Suhrkamp, 1970), 58–80; Kenley Royce Dove, "Logik und Recht bei Hegel," *Neue Hefte für Philosophie* 17 (1979): 89–108; Manfred Hanisch, *Dialektische Logik und politisches Argument: Untersuchungen zu den methodischen Grundlagen der Hegelschen*

Staatsphilosophie (Königstein: Forum Academicum, 1981); Heinz Kimmerle, "'Wissenschaft der Logik' als Grundlegung seines Systems der Philosophie: Über das Verhältnis von 'Logik' und 'Realphilosophie,'" in *Die Logik des Wissens und das Problem der Erziehung*, ed. Wilhelm Raimund Beyer (Hamburg: Felix Meiner, 1982), 52–60; Henning Ottmann, "Hegelsche Logik und Rechtsphilosophie: Unzulängliche Bemerkungen zu einem ungelösten Problem," in *Hegels Philosophie des Rechts: Die Theorie der Rechtsformen*, ed. Dieter Henrich and Rolf-Peter Horstmann (Stuttgart: Klett-Cotta, 1982), 382–91; and Denis L. Rosenfield, *Politique et liberté: Une étude sur la structure logique de la Philosophie du droit de Hegel* (Paris: Aubier, 1984).

Chapter 2

1. On this point, see Charles Taylor, "Hegel and the Philosophy of Action," in *Hegel's Philosophy of Action*, ed. Lawrence S. Stepelevich and David Lamb (Atlantic Highlands, N.J.: Humanities, 1983), 1–18.

2. I adopt here a version of the classification of current interpretations proposed by Alan Patten in his *Hegel's Idea of Freedom* (Oxford: Oxford University Press, 1999), chap. 1.

Patten includes discussion of a fourth paradigm, what he calls the "metaphysical reading," which he associates with the work of Charles Taylor, that sees human freedom as an expression of the historical self-realization of the divine. I leave this particular paradigm aside since I do not believe it to be faithful to Hegel's own thought and, more importantly, it plays little role in the current approach to Hegel's theory of freedom.

3. The most famous formulation of this view comes from F. H. Bradley's "My Station and Its Duties" in his *Ethical Studies* (London: Henry King, 1876).

4. The best accounts of the self-actualization reading are Joachim Ritter, *Metaphysik und Politik: Studien zu Aristoteles und Hegel;* and Allen W. Wood, *Hegel's Ethical Thought.*

5. The most influential and substantial presentation of this approach is to be found in a series of works by Robert Pippin: *Modernism as a Philosophical Problem* (Oxford: Blackwell, 1991) and *Idealism as Modernism: Hegelian Variations* (Cambridge: Cambridge University Press, 1997).

6. Note that the claim here is not that any of these paradigms ultimately proposes to conceive of freedom in Hegel as merely choice, but that they take this conception as basic, for varying reasons, and, in doing so, render the accounts they build upon this basis necessarily vulnerable to skeptical attack.

7. It has become common to employ the notion of mindedness or even likemindedness to try to capture the sense of Hegel's concept of *Geist*. I refrain from taking this path for two reasons. First, Hegel is clear, here and elsewhere, that the concept refers, fundamentally, to a process, a kind of revealing or appearing, rather than an epistemic capacity. Secondly, defining *Geist* in terms of mindedness threatens to restrict the sense of this notion to only one of its more highly determinate forms, namely consciousness.

8. A compatibilist version of the relationship of nature and spirit has been proposed, in divergent ways, by Richard Schacht, "Hegel on Freedom," in *Hegel: A Collection of Critical Essays*, ed. Alasdair MacIntyre (New York: Anchor Books, 19672), 289–328; G. H. R. Parkinson, "Hegel's Concept of Freedom," in *Hegel*,

ed. Michael Inwood (Oxford: Oxford University Press, 1985), 153–73; and Robert Pippin, "Hegel, Freedom, the Will, *The Philosophy of Right* (§§1–33)," in *G. W. F. Hegel: Grundlinien der Philosophie des Rechts*, ed. Ludwig Siep (Berlin: Akademie Verlag, 1997), 31–53, esp. 37–44, and in Pippin's *Hegel's Practical Philosophy*, chap. 2.

9. This way of defining *Geist* obviously opens the question of the status of nonhuman animals: would such organisms, in Hegel's theory, count as spiritual beings? Clearly, this important question is beyond the scope of the present study. But it should be noted that Hegel's system does adamantly root all the more determinate forms of spirit in this fundamental kind of self-relation that is a registering by a natural organism of nothing more than its own corporeal integrity within its environment.

10. It is worth noting here that Hegel's account of purposes and intentions at *GPR* §§115–28 is, in the interpretation proposed here, an examination of higher-order determinations of the ends and purposes discussed here.

11. In what follows, I focus exclusively on the account of *practical* freedom in Hegel's system, leaving aside its various other senses and the domains in which it is discussed. For discussion of these broader dimensions of Hegel's project, see Wolfgang Marx, "Die Logik des Freiheitsbegriffs," *Hegel-Studien*, vol. 11 (1976): 125–48; Angehrn, *Freiheit und System bei Hegel*; and Will Dudley, *Hegel, Nietzsche, and Philosophy: Thinking Freedom* (Cambridge: Cambridge University Press, 2002), chaps. 1–4.

12. Several studies of Hegel's theory of freedom have analyzed what they take to be its "dual nature" (Neuhouser, *Foundations of Hegel's Social Theory*) or its "psychological and social dimensions" (Pippin, *Hegel's Practical Philosophy*). The conditions outlined here seek to go further by spelling out the terms that acts must satisfy in order to count as genuinely free acts.

13. For an extended discussion of the logical structure of the free will, see Klaus Vieweg, *Das Denken der Freiheit: Hegels Grundlinien der Philosophie des Rechts* (Munich: Wilhelm Fink, 2011), 57–96.

14. On this crucial point, see Stephen Houlgate, "The Unity of Theoretical and Practical Spirit in Hegel's Concept of Freedom," *Review of Metaphysics* 48, no. 4 (1995): 859–81; Peperzak, *Modern Freedom*, 168–73; and Thomas A. Lewis, *Freedom and Tradition in Hegel: Reconsidering Anthropology, Ethics, and Religion* (Notre Dame, Ind.: Notre Dame University Press, 2005), chap. 4.

15. Very little research has been done on Hegel's psychology and its relationship to his account of the will. See the pioneering work of Adriaan Peperzak, "The Foundations of Ethics According to Hegel," *International Philosophical Quarterly* 23, no. 4 (1983): 349–65; and his *Hegels praktische Philosophie: Ein Kommentar zur enzyklopädischen Darstellung der menschlichen Freiheit und ihrer objektiven Verwirklichung* (Stuttgart-Bad Cannstatt: Frommann-Holzboog, 1991), chap. 1.

More recently, see Lewis, *Freedom and Tradition in Hegel*, 96–113; and Christopher Yeomans, "'Acting On' Instead of 'Stepping Back': Hegel's Conception of the Relation between Motivations and the Free Will," in *Yo y Tiempo. La antropología filosófica de G.W.F. Hegel, vol. I: La sustancialidad y subjetividad humanas*, ed. I. Falgueras, J. A. García, and Juan J. Padial, *Contrastes*, Suplemento 15 (2010): 377–87.

16. The nature of the contradiction inherent in *Willkür* has been noted by others. See Robert Theis, "Volonté et liberté: Commentaire de l'Introduction à la Philosophie du Droit de Hegel," *Archiv für Rechts- und Sozialphilosophie* 65, no. 3 (1979): 369–86, esp. 377–81; Donald J. Maletz, "The Meaning of 'Will' in Hegel's *Philosophy of Right*," *Interpretation* 13, no. 2 (1985): 195–212, esp. 205–7; Parkinson, "Hegel's Concept of Freedom," 159–61; Wood, *Hegel's Ethical Thought*, 58–60; Peperzak, *Modern Freedom*, 203–7; and, most extensively perhaps, Christopher Yeomans, *Freedom and Reflection: Hegel on the Logic of Agency* (Oxford: Oxford University Press, 2012), 167–75.

17. My contention is that in his treatment of the problem of the measure, Hegel is addressing the need for a criterion of autonomous action that would be, at once, a *principium diiudicationis bonitatis* (a principle of good judgment) and a *principium executionis bonitatis* (a principle of good action).

On this historical problem and how it shaped Kant's practical philosophy and the work of those who followed in his wake, see Dieter Henrich, "Ethik der Autonomie," in his *Selbstverhältnisse: Gedanken und Auslegungen zu den Grundlagen der klassischen deutschen Philosophie* (Stuttgart: Philipp Reclam, 1982), 6–56.

18. On the important point that desires are motivational for Hegel only insofar as they are justified as well, see Patten, *Hegel's Idea of Freedom*, 55–57.

19. On the distinctive character of Hegel's concept of happiness, see Wood, *Hegel's Ethical Thought*, 60–69; see also, Neuhouser, *Foundations of Hegel's Social Theory*, 167.

20. Allen Wood distinguishes two lines of argument in Hegel's account of the relationship of happiness and freedom. The first is the indeterminacy argument, which holds that the very concept of happiness itself is indeterminate, while the second, the priority argument, holds that freedom is more fundamental than happiness because desires are ultimately pursued, for Hegel, only for the sake of being a coherent whole expression of the self. See his *Hegel's Ethical Thought*, 63–71.

On the interpretation that I propose here, the indeterminacy of happiness is what necessarily entails that its truth, which is to say, its ground, lies in freedom. I believe this reading better captures the actual line of argument as it is set out in the text, and it is more cogent philosophically than the rather forced version that Wood proposes (see *Hegel's Ethical Thought*, esp. 69–70).

21. I draw here upon Wood's excellent exposition of *bei sich selbst*; see his *Hegel's Ethical Thought*, 45–47.

22. It is important to note that, on the reading proposed here, Hegel's account holds genuinely free acts to be natural processes, but ones that are distinctly not reducible to this dimension. Hegel thus works, as noted above, outside the parameters of the classic compatibilist/non-compatibilist debates. Nature and spirit are one, but are not reducible to one another.

Chapter 3

1. On the development of the concept of Objective Spirit in Hegel's thought, see Franz Rosenzweig, *Hegel und der Staat*, ed. Frank Lachmann (1920; Frankfurt am Main: Suhrkamp, 2010), 359–67; Jacques D'Hondt, "Genèse et structure de l'unité de l'Esprit Objectif," in *Hegel: L'Esprit Objectif / L'Unité de l'Histoire*

(Lille: Association des Publications de la Faculté des Lettres et Sciences Humaines de Lille, 1970), 99–112; and Jean-François Kervégan, "Die Objektivität des Objektiven Geistes," in *Geist: Erkundungen zu einem Begriff*, ed. Andres Arndt and Jure Zovko (Hannover: Wehrhahn, 2009), 63–81.

For the significance of the concept within the context of the history of political thought, see Manfred Riedel, "Framework and Meaning of 'Objective Spirit': A Conceptual Change in Political Philosophy," in his *Between Tradition & Revolution: The Hegelian Transformation of Political Philosophy*, trans. Walter Wright (Cambridge: Cambridge University Press, 1984), 3–30.

On the place of Objective Spirit within the system of philosophical sciences, see Angehrn, *Freiheit und System bei Hegel*, 153–61; Vittorio Hösle, "Die Stellung von Hegels Philosophie des objektiven Geistes in seinem System und ihre Aporie," in *Anspruch und Leistung von Hegels Rechtsphilosophie*, ed. Christoph Jermann (Stuttgart-Bad Cannstatt: Frommann-Holzboog, 1987), 11–53; and Adriaan Peperzak, *Selbsterkenntnis des Absoluten: Grundlinien der Hegelschen Philosophie des Geistes* (Stuttgart-Bad Cannstatt: Frommann-Holzboog, 1987), chap. 3.

2. Hegel refers to "second nature" in both an objective and a subjective sense. For the objective sense, where it designates institutions, forms of life, and social relations, see *GPR* §151. For the subjective sense, where the phrase refers to stable dispositions, capacities, and attitudes, see, though the term itself is not used in the first edition of the *Encyclopedia*, the account of habit at *Enz. 1817*, §325.

For consideration of "second nature" in relationship to Objective Spirit, see Manfred Riedel, "Laws of Nature and Laws of Right: Problems in the Realization of Freedom," in his *Between Tradition & Revolution*, 57–75, esp. 59–64; and Adriaan Peperzak, "'Second Nature': Place and Significance of the Objective Spirit in Hegel's Encyclopedia," *The Owl of Minerva* 27, no. 1 (fall 1995): 51–66.

For the rich history of the concept, see Gerhard Funke, "Natur, zweite (I)," in *Historisches Wörterbuch der Philosophie*, vol. 6 (Basel: Schwabe, 1984), 484–89; and Norbert Rath, "Natur, zweite (II)," in *Historisches Wörterbuch der Philosophie*, vol. 6, 489–94, and also his *Zweite Natur: Konzepte einer Vermittlung von Natur und Kultur in Anthropologie und Ästhetik um 1800* (Münster: Waxmann, 1996).

3. Nicolai Hartmann, *Philosophie des deutschen Idealismus*, 2nd ed. (Berlin: Walter de Gruyter, 1960), 496 (emphases added).

4. Charles Taylor, *Hegel* (Cambridge: Cambridge University Press, 1975), esp. 478–88. This model has been taken up more recently in a more sophisticated and nuanced version in the semantic inferentialism of Robert Brandom (see his *Making It Explicit: Reasoning, Representing, and Discursive Commitment* [Cambridge, Mass.: Harvard University Press, 1994]) and in the holism of Vincent Descombes (*The Institutions of Meaning: A Defense of Anthropological Holism* [Cambridge, Mass.: Harvard University Press, 2014], chap. 10).

5. Axel Honneth, *Kampf um Anerkennung: Zur moralischen Grammatik sozialer Konflikte* (Frankfurt am Main: Suhrkamp, 1994); and, more recently, see his explicit attempt to work out a critical appropriation, or what he calls a "reactualization," of Hegel's political philosophy in *Leiden an Unbestimmtheit: Eine Reaktualisierung der Hegelschen Rechtsphilosophie* (Stuttgart: Philipp Reclam, 2001). This model is largely endorsed, with some important caveats, by the social agency theory of Robert Pippin; see his *Hegel's Practical Philosophy*, esp. part 3.

6. On the concept of right at work in the late Romantic Historical School of Hugo and Savigny, see Elisabeth Weisser-Lohmann, *Rechtsphilosophie als praktiche Philosophie: Hegels Grundlinien der Philosophie des Rechts und die Grundlegung der praktischen Philosophie* (Munich: Wilhelm Fink, 2011), 74–87.

7. For a discussion of Hegel in relation to the "natural right" tradition, see Norberto Bobbio, "Hegel und die Naturrechtslehre," in *Materialien zu Hegels Rechtsphilosophie*, vol. 2, ed. Manfred Riedel (Frankfurt am Main: Suhrkamp, 1974), 81–108; Manfred Riedel, "Laws of Nature and Laws of Right," in his *Between Tradition & Revolution*, 57–75; and Montserrat Herreo, "The Right of Freedom regarding Nature in Hegel's *Philosophy of Right*," in *Contemporary Perspectives on Natural Law: Natural Law as a Limiting Concept*, ed. Ana Marta González (London: Routledge, 2008), 141–60.

8. It is worth noting here that the *Elements of the Philosophy of Right* is actually only one of the two titles that Hegel gave the text that we are discussing. The other, appearing originally on the left-hand page opposite the better-known title, was *Naturrecht und Staatswisssenschaft im Grundrisse: Zum Gebrauch für seine Vorlesungen* (*Natural Right and Political Science in Outline: For Use in His Lectures*). Hegel is clearly making use of the term *Naturrecht* here in this title in the latter sense referred to at *Enz. 1817*, §415A: right as "determined by the nature of the matter, that is, by the *concept*." I seek to explain what that sense means in the account of Objective Spirit and Right that follows.

9. The approach taken to this question in what follows is closest to that developed by Jean-François Kervégan in "Le Droit entre Nature et Histoire: Hegel," in *Recht zwischen Natur und Geschichte / Le Droit entre nature et histoire*, ed. Jean-François Kervégan and Heinz Mohnhaupt (Frankfurt am Main: Vittorio Klostermann, 1997), 223–56.

10. In his discussion of the senses of objectivity at *GPR* §26, Frederick Neuhouser claims that the will wholly immersed in its object, the second sense of objective will set out in the paragraph, also plays a role in Hegel's account insofar as individuals can be free, albeit in a limited sense, "simply in virtue of inhabiting an inherently rational (objectively free) social world, regardless of their subjective relation to the laws and institutions of that world" (Neuhouser, *Foundations of Hegel's Social Theory*, 117). While I agree with this point and believe that it is faithful to Hegel's theory, it does not, I argue, play a direct role in defining the twofold sense of objectivity to which Hegel is appealing at *GPR* §27.

11. The normative ontological account of institutions for which I argue here disagrees with Benno Zabel's proposal that institutions, for Hegel, are best understood as "praxis forms," that is, as cultures of intersubjective recognition, and as "legal forms," structures establishing status and guaranteeing freedom, since these notions fail to capture, I believe, the way in which the social and political institutions of right are ontologically objective precisely in the sense of "immediate actuality" to which Hegel refers at *GPR* §27. See Benno Zabel, "The Institutional Turn in Hegel's Philosophy of Right: Towards a Conception of Freedom beyond Individualism and Collectivism," *Hegel Bulletin*, 36, no. 1 (2015): 80–104, esp. 86–89.

12. Accordingly, the intertwined accounts of Objective Spirit, Right, and *Sittlichkeit* (Ethicality) that follow hold Hegel's theory to be a distinctive form of

institutionalism. In this respect, they follow a line of interpretation first proposed by Dieter Henrich. Henrich argues that Hegel's political theory is a form of what he calls "robust [*starken*] institutionalism," which teaches that "the freedom of the individual will can only be realized in an order that, as itself objective, has the form of the rational will and thus includes the individual will entirely within itself, subsuming it under its own conditions, as always without alienation" ("Vernunft in Verwirklichung," 31)

While endorsing the basic institutionalist approach that Henrich outlines, Jean-François Kervégan has criticized Henrich's version for subordinating the will of the individual wholly and completely to the institutional structures whereby it is enabled to be free. Kervégan thus argues for a more moderate "weak [*faible*] institutionalism" in its stead (see his *L'Effectif et le rationnel*, 311–14 and 366–71; on this point, see also, Wood, *Hegel's Ethical Thought*, 73–74).

13. The adjective *heilig* is derived from the same root as the verb *heilen*: to heal, to cure, to redeem, to make whole.

14. It is worth noting here that, though Morality is a higher form of right than Abstract Right, this does not entail that any *singular* moral intention can justify violating the norms of ownership and contract (see *GPR* §126).

This is distinct from the issue of the "right of necessity," which involves the whole of one's very existence, that brings the inherent conflict between the domains of Abstract Right and Morality to the fore. We will consider this right in some detail in what follows.

15. The term is ill-chosen here since in the next paragraph, that is, at *GPR* §32 and A (see also, *GPR* §3A), Hegel clearly distinguishes between conceptual determinations (*Bestimmungen*) of right and their historical shapes (*Gestaltungen*). The determinations follow the systematic development of the concept of freedom that we studied in chapter 2, rather than any historical sequence. The science of right is thus, as we have argued, a distinctly systematic discipline, rather than some form of historical investigation.

16. See the excellent examination of this right and the account of the argument that Hegel mounts around it in Peperzak, *Modern Freedom*, 348–60. See also Henrich, "Vernunft in Verwirklichung," 18–23, esp. 20–21; Wolfgang Schild, "Hegels Lehre vom Notrecht," in *Die Rechtsphilosophie des Deutschen Idealismus*, ed. Vittorio Hösle (Hamburg: Meiner, 1989), 146–63; and Domenico Losurdo, *Hegel and the Freedom of Moderns*, trans. Marella Morris and Jon Morris (Durham, N.C.: Duke University Press, 2004), chap. 7.

17. It should be noted that the issue of relative deprivation and its relationship to right that is at the core of the question of a right of necessity does reemerge in the account of Ethicality. Initially, it appears in the form of the problem of poverty (*GPR* §§241–43) and then in the problem of the formation of a group that, beyond simply the inequities of the distribution of goods, exhibits a common disposition of disaffection, estrangement, or alienation from right itself, a group that Hegel refers to as the "rabble [*Pöbel*]" (*GPR* §§244–48).

These issues and whether or not the science of right is able to address them adequately are, of course, beyond the purview of the present study.

18. A neglected, but excellent example of this now fairly conventional way of understanding Hegel's overarching argument is W. H. Walsh, *Hegelian Ethics* (London: Macmillan, 1969).

19. Though crucial, this inference is generally neglected in the scholarly literature. Three important examples are the following.

Instead of grappling with the actual terms of the transition, Joachim Ritter appeals to the idea that Hegel seeks here to sublate the Kantian moral standpoint, which he takes Morality to articulate, by the "'ethical' constitution of the free life of citizens constitutive for the Greek world" (*Hegel and the French Revolution: Essays on The Philosophy of Right*, trans. Richard Dien Winfield [Cambridge, Mass.: MIT Press, 1982], 162).

In his account of this transition, Ludwig Siep concludes that various aspects of Morality are "criticized, 'conserved,' and transposed to various degrees" in the determinate duties of a specific community of human beings without explaining the necessity behind this claim. See his "The 'Aufhebung' of Morality in Ethical Life," in *Hegel's Philosophy of Action*, 137–55.

Finally, in otherwise excellent accounts of Morality and Ethical Life, Allen Wood never explicitly addresses the transition from the former to the latter, other than to say that the relation between them is a "complex one" ("Hegel's Critique of Morality," in *G. W. F. Hegel: Grundlinien der Philosophie des Rechts*, 165; see also his *Hegel's Ethical Thought*, chaps. 9–11).

Klaus Vieweg, on the other hand, provides an extensive analysis of the argument of *GPR* §141 and helpfully compares it with the transition from Abstract Right to Morality. See his *Das Denken der Freiheit*, 223–28.

20. At *Enz. 1817*, §429, Hegel had already formulated, at least in outline, an extremely compressed version of the argument he develops in *GPR* §141:

The pure abstract good disposition [*Gesinnung*] is, within its own self [*innerhalb ihrer selbst*], the sublation [*Aufheben*] of the mediation of this reflection and choosing in the simple universality of the good—the nothingness of what is nothing. This universality has, at the same time, in its concept and in this consciousness, the meaning of the unsayable or the completely immediate good—thus, the objective. Subjectivity, in this its own identity with the objective, has thus sublated [*aufgehoben*] the standpoint of relations, and has passed into ethicality [*Sittlichkeit*].

Conclusion

1. For the history of the development and publication of this text, see the invaluable study by Hans-Christian Lucas and Udo Rameil, "Furcht vor der Zensur: Zur Enstehungs- und Druckgeschichte von Hegels Grundlinien der Philosophie ds Rechts," *Hegel-Studien* 15 (1980): 63–93; for evidence for the claim that the book was available by October 1820, see 90–93.

2. Paulus was a fellow graduate of the Tübingen Seminary and a colleague of Hegel's in Jena, and he served as the school commissioner to whom Hegel reported as rector of the Gymnasium in Nuremberg; he was also one of those responsible for Hegel's invitation to join the faculty at Heidelberg. They finally broke, however, over Hegel's support of the king's position in the Württemberg constitutional debates of 1816–17.

On this last aspect of the relationship, see Terry Pinkard, *Hegel: A Biography* (Cambridge: Cambridge University Press, 2000), 408–11.

3. For Paulus's review, which originally appeared in the *Heidelberger Jahrbücher der Literatur*, see *Materialien zu Hegels Rechtsphilosophie*, ed. Manfred

Riedel, vol. 1, 53–66; for his account of the tension between is and ought, see, in particular, 57–60 and 63.

4. For an excellent example of this approach, see Beiser, *Enlightenment, Revolution, & Romanticism.*

5. For a detailed history of these issues and the various interpretations to which they have given rise, see Henning Ottmann, *Individuum und Gemeinschaft bei Hegel, Band I: Hegel in Spiegel der Interpretationen.* For a concise account in English of these charges, see M. W. Jackson, "Hegel: The Real and the Rational," in *The Hegel Myths and Legends*, ed. Jon Stewart (Evanston, Ill.: Northwestern University Press, 1996), 19–25.

6. Ernst Tugendhat, *Self-Consciousness and Self-Determination*, trans. Paul Stern (Cambridge, Mass.: MIT Press, 1986), 317.

7. See Eric Weil, *Hegel and the State*, trans. Mark A. Cohen (Baltimore, Md.: Johns Hopkins University Press, 1998); and Jacques D'Hondt, *Hegel in His Time: Berlin, 1818–1831*, trans. John Burbidge, Nelson Roland, and Judith Levasseur (Peterborough, Ont.: Broadview, 1988).

8. I hold this to be the principal failing of Hans-Friedrich Fulda's otherwise magisterial study, *Das Recht der Philosophie in Hegels Philosophie des Rechts* (Frankfurt am Main: Vittorio Klostermann, 1968).

9. Though ultimately the proposals differ quite fundamentally, Andrew Buchwalter's account of what he calls the immanent and transcendent dimensions of Hegel's normative theory is, I believe, grappling with many of the same issues as the account that follows and its distinctions between the systematic and extra-systematic usages of reason and the necessary entwining of systematicity and representation that this entails.

For Buchwalter's interpretation, see his *Dialectics, Politics, and the Contemporary Value of Hegel's Practical Philosophy* (New York: Routledge, 2012), 9–14 and 41–82.

10. For an excellent explication of these passages that reconstructs the sometimes dense historical and intellectual contexts to which they refer, see Adriaan Peperzak, *Philosophy and Politics: A Commentary on the Preface to Hegel's Philosophy of Right* (Dordrecht: Martinus Nijhoff, 1987), 64–92.

11. On the relevant secondary literature and the rather complex issues they raise regarding the question of the metaphor of the rose and the cross, see Peperzak, *Philosophy and Politics*, 108–12.

12. For the decisive role of Luther in Hegel's conception of the historical role of his thought, and in particular the idea of a second reformation—one not just of doctrine (*Lehre*) but of life (*Leben*) as well—as one of its underlying themes, see Laurence Dickey, *Hegel: Religion, Economics, and the Politics of Spirit, 1770–1807* (Cambridge: Cambridge University Press, 1987); Dickey, "Hegel on Religion and Philosophy," in *The Cambridge Companion to Hegel*, ed. Frederick C. Beiser (Cambridge: Cambridge University Press, 1993), 301–34, and finally, Dickey's "General Introduction," in *Hegel: Political Writings*, ed. Laurence Dickey, trans. H. B. Nisbet (Cambridge: Cambridge University Press, 1999), vii–xxxiii.

13. On the importance of the emergence of a pietist form of Lutheranism in shaping Hegel's early thought, see Dickey, *Hegel: Religion, Economics, and the Politics of Spirit, 1770–1807*, part 1 and, on Arndt, in particular, 61–76.

For historical accounts of the growth of pietism in the context of Lutheranism, see F. E. Stoeffler, *The Rise of Evangelical Pietism* (Leiden: Brill, 1965); and, more broadly, Ernst Troeltsch, *The Social Teaching of the Christian Churches*, vol. 2 (London: George Allen and Unwin, 1931), 515–75.

BIBLIOGRAPHY

Angehrn, Emil. *Freiheit und System bei Hegel.* Berlin: Walter de Gruyter, 1977.

Aretin, Karl Otmar Freiherr von, ed. *Der Aufgeklärte Absolutismus.* Cologne: Kiepenheuer and Witsch, 1974.

Baxa, Jakob. *Einführung in die romantische Staatswissenschaft.* Jena: Fischer, 1923.

Beiser, Frederick C. *Enlightenment, Revolution, & Romanticism: The Genesis of Modern German Political Thought, 1790–1800.* Cambridge, Mass.: Harvard University Press, 1992.

———. "Two Concepts of Reason in German Idealism." In *Internationales Jahrbuch des Deutschen Idealismus (2003) / International Yearbook of German Idealism (2003): Konzepte der Rationalität / Concepts of Rationality,* 13–27. Berlin: Walter de Gruyter, 2002.

Berman, Robert. "Categorial Justification: Normative Argumentation in Hegel's Practical Philosophy," Ph.D. dissertation, New School Graduate Faculty, August 1982.

Bobbio, Norberto. "Hegel und die Naturrechtslehre." In *Materialien zu Hegels Rechtsphilosophie,* edited by Manfred Riedel, vol. 2: 81–108. Frankfurt am Main: Suhrkamp, 1974.

Bradley, F. H. "My Station and Its Duties." In his *Ethical Studies.* London: Henry King, 1876.

Brandom, Robert. *Making It Explicit: Reasoning, Representing, and Discursive Commitment.* Cambridge, Mass.: Harvard University Press, 1994.

Brooks, Thom. *Hegel's Political Philosophy: A Systematic Reading of the Philosophy of Right.* Edinburgh: Edinburgh University Press, 2007.

Buchwalter, Andrew. *Dialectics, Politics, and the Contemporary Value of Hegel's Practical Philosophy.* New York: Routledge, 2012.

Collins, Ardis B. *Hegel's Phenomenology: The Dialectical Justification of Philosophy's First Principles.* Montreal: McGill-Queen's University Press, 2013.

Descombes, Vincent. *The Institutions of Meaning: A Defense of Anthropological Holism.* Cambridge, Mass.: Harvard University Press, 2014.

D'Hondt, Jacques. "Genèse et structure de l'unité de l'Esprit Objectif." In *Hegel: L'Esprit Objectif / L'Unité de l'Histoire,* 99–112. Lille: Association des Publications de la Faculté des Lettres et Sciences Humaines de Lille, 1970.

———. *Hegel in His Time: Berlin, 1818–1831,* translated by John Burbidge, Nelson Roland, and Judith Levasseur. Peterborough, Ont.: Broadview, 1988.

Dickey, Laurence. "General Introduction." In *Hegel: Political Writings,* edited by Laurence Dickey, translated by H. B. Nisbet, vii–xxxiii. Cambridge: Cambridge University Press, 1999.

———. "Hegel on Religion and Philosophy." In *The Cambridge Companion to Hegel,* edited by Frederick C. Beiser, 301–34. Cambridge: Cambridge University Press, 1993.

———. *Hegel: Religion, Economics, and the Politics of Spirit, 1770–1807.* Cambridge: Cambridge University Press, 1987.

Dove, Kenley Royce. "Logik und Recht bei Hegel." *Neue Hefte für Philosophie* 17 (1979): 89–108.

Droz, Jacques. *Le Romantisme allemand et l'état.* Paris: Payot, 1966.

Dudley, Will. *Hegel, Nietzsche, and Philosophy: Thinking Freedom.* Cambridge: Cambridge University Press, 2002.

Epstein, Klaus. *The Genesis of German Conservatism.* Princeton, N.J.: Princeton University Press, 1966.

Franks, Paul W. *All or Nothing: Systematicity, Transcendental Arguments, and Skepticism in German Idealism.* Cambridge, Mass.: Harvard University Press, 2005.

Fulda, Hans-Friedrich. *Das Recht der Philosophie in Hegels Philosophie des Rechts.* Frankfurt am Main: Vittorio Klostermann, 1968.

———. "Zum Theorietypus der Hegelschen Rechtsphilosophie." In *Hegels Philosophie des Rechts*, edited by Henrich and Horstmann, 393–427. Stuttgart: Klett-Cotta, 1982.

Funke, Gerhard. "Natur, zweite (I)." In *Historisches Wörterbuch der Philosophie*, vol. 6: 484–89. Basel: Schwabe, 1984.

Hanisch, Manfred. *Dialektische Logik und politisches Argument: Untersuchungen zu den methodischen Grundlagen der Hegelschen Staatsphilosophie.* Königstein: Forum Academicum, 1981.

Hardimon, Michael O. *Hegel's Social Philosophy: The Project of Reconciliation.* Cambridge: Cambridge University Press, 1994.

Hartmann, Klaus. "Ideen zu einem neuen systematischen Verständnis der Hegelschen Rechtsphilosophie." *Perspektiven der Philosophie* 2 (1976): 167–200.

Hartmann, Nicolai. *Philosophie des deutschen Idealismus.* 2nd edition. Berlin: Walter de Gruyter, 1960.

Henrich, Dieter. "Ethik der Autonomie." In his *Selbstverhältnisse: Gedanken und Auslegungen zu den Grundlagen der klassischen deutschen Philosophie,* 6–56. Stuttgart: Philipp Reclam, 1982.

———. "Vernunft in Verwirklichung." In Georg Friedrich Wilhelm Hegel, *Philosophie des Rechts: Die Vorlesung von 1819/20 in einer Nachschrift*, edited by Dieter Henrich, 9–39. Frankfurt am Main: Suhrkamp, 1982.

Henrich, Dieter, and Rolf-Peter Horstmann, eds. *Hegels Philosophie des Rechts: Die Theorie der Rechtsformen.* Stuttgart: Klett-Cotta, 1982.

Herreo, Montserrat. "The Right of Freedom Regarding Nature in Hegel's *Philosophy of Right.*" In *Contemporary Perspectives on Natural Law: Natural Law as a Limiting Concept*, edited by Ana Marta González, 141–60. London: Routledge, 2008.

Honneth, Axel. *Kampf um Anerkennung: Zur moralischen Grammatik sozialer Konflikte.* Frankfurt am Main: Suhrkamp, 1994.

———. *Leiden an Unbestimmtheit: Eine Reaktualisierung der Hegelschen Rechtsphilosophie.* Stuttgart: Philipp Reclam, 2001.

Hösle, Vittorio. "Die Stellung von Hegels Philosophie des objektiven Geistes in seinem System und ihre Aporie." In *Anspruch und Leistung von Hegels Rechtsphilosophie*, edited by Christoph Jermann, 11–53. Stuttgart-Bad Cannstatt: Frommann-Holzboog, 1987.

———. *Hegels System: Der Idealismus der Subjektivität und das Problem der Intersubjektivität.* Hamburg: Felix Meiner, 1988.

Houlgate, Stephen. *The Opening of Hegel's Logic: From Being to Infinity.* West Lafayette, Ind.: Purdue University Press, 2006.

———. "The Unity of Theoretical and Practical Spirit in Hegel's Concept of Freedom." *Review of Metaphysics* 48, no. 4 (1995): 859–81.

Jackson, M. W. "Hegel: The Real and the Rational." In *The Hegel Myths and Legends*, edited by Jon Stewart, 19–25. Evanston, Ill.: Northwestern University Press, 1996.

Ilting, Karl-Heinz. "Rechtsphilosophie als Phänomenologie des Bewusstseins der Freiheit." In *Hegels Philosophie des Rechts*, edited by Henrich and Horstmann, 225–54. Stuttgart: Klett-Cotta, 1982.

Kervégan, Jean-François. "Die Objektivität des Objektiven Geistes." In *Geist: Erkundungen zu einem Begriff*, edited by Andres Arndt and Jure Zovko, 63–81. Hannover: Wehrhahn, 2009.

———. "Le Droit entre Nature et Histoire: Hegel." In *Recht zwischen Natur und Geschichte / Le Droit entre nature et histoire*, edited by Jean-François Kervégan and Heinz Mohnhaupt, 223–56. Frankfurt am Main: Vittorio Klostermann, 1997.

———. *L'Effectif et le rationnel: Hegel et l'esprit objectif.* Paris: Vrin, 2007.

Kimmerle, Heinz. "'Wissenschaft der Logik' als Grundlegung seines Systems der Philosophie: Über das Verhältnis von 'Logik' und 'Realphilosophie.'" In *Die Logik des Wissens und das Problem der Erziehung*, edited by Wilhelm Raimund Beyer, 52–60. Hamburg: Felix Meiner, 1982.

Kopitzsch, Franklin, ed. *Aufklärung, Absolutismus und Bürgertum in Deutschland.* Munich: Nymphenburger Verlagshandlung, 1976.

Krieger, Leonard. *An Essay on the Theory of Enlightened Despotism.* Chicago: University of Chicago Press, 1975.

Lewis, Thomas A. *Freedom and Tradition in Hegel: Reconsidering Anthropology, Ethics, and Religion.* Notre Dame, Ind.: Notre Dame University Press, 2005.

Losurdo, Domenico. *Hegel and the Freedom of Moderns*, translated by Marella Morris and Jon Morris. Durham, N.C.: Duke University Press, 2004.

Lucas, Hans-Christian, and Udo Rameil. "Furcht vor der Zensur: Zur Enstehungs- und Druckgeschichte von Hegels Grundlinien der Philosophie des Rechts," *Hegel-Studien* 15 (1980): 63–93.

Maletz, Donald J. "The Meaning of 'Will' in Hegel's *Philosophy of Right.*" *Interpretation* 13, no. 2 (1985): 195–212.

Marx, Wolfgang. "Die Logik des Freiheitsbegriffs." *Hegel-Studien*, vol. 11 (1976): 125–48.

Neuhouser, Frederick. *Foundations of Hegel's Social Theory: Actualizing Freedom.* Cambridge, Mass.: Harvard University Press, 2000.

Nuzzo, Angelica. *System.* Bielefeld: Transcript Verlag, 2003.

Ottmann, Henning. "Hegelsche Logik und Rechtsphilosophie. Unzulängliche Bemerkungen zu einem ungelösten Problem." In *Hegels Philosophie des Rechts*, edited by Henrich and Horstmann, 382–91. Stuttgart: Klett-Cotta, 1982.

———. *Individuum und Gemeinschaft bei Hegel, Band I: Hegel im Spiegel der Interpretationen.* Berlin: Walter de Gruyter, 1977.

Parkinson, G. H. R. "Hegel's Concept of Freedom." In *Hegel*, edited by Michael Inwood, 153–73. Oxford: Oxford University Press, 1985.

Patten, Alan. *Hegel's Idea of Freedom.* Oxford: Oxford University Press, 1999.

Peperzak, Adriaan T. "The Foundations of Ethics According to Hegel." *International Philosophical Quarterly* 23, no. 4 (1983): 349–65.

———. *Hegels praktische Philosophie: Ein Kommentar zur enzyklopädischen Darstellung der menschlichen Freiheit und ihrer objektiven Verwirklichung.* Stuttgart-Bad Cannstatt: Frommann-Holzboog, 1991.

———. *Modern Freedom: Hegel's Legal, Moral, and Political Philosophy.* Dordrecht: Kluwer Academic, 2001.

———. *Philosophy and Politics: A Commentary on the Preface to Hegel's Philosophy of Right.* Dordrecht: Martinus Nijhoff, 1987.

———. "'Second Nature': Place and Significance of the Objective Spirit in Hegel's Encyclopedia." *The Owl of Minerva* 27, no. 1 (fall 1995): 51–66.

———. *Selbsterkenntnis des Absoluten: Grundlinien der Hegelschen Philosophie des Geistes.* Stuttgart-Bad Cannstatt: Frommann-Holzboog, 1987.

Pinkard, Terry. "Freedom and Social Categories." *Philosophy and Phenomenological Research* 47 (1986): 209–32.

———. *Hegel: A Biography.* Cambridge: Cambridge University Press, 2000.

Pippin, Robert. "Hegel, Freedom, the Will, *The Philosophy of Right* (§§1–33)." In *G. W. F. Hegel: Grundlinien der Philosophie des Rechts*, edited by Ludwig Siep, 31–53. Berlin: Akademie Verlag, 1997.

———. *Hegel's Practical Philosophy: Rational Agency as Ethical Life.* Cambridge: Cambridge University Press, 2008.

———. *Idealism as Modernism: Hegelian Variations.* Cambridge: Cambridge University Press, 1997.

———. *Modernism as a Philosophical Problem.* Oxford: Blackwell, 1991.

Rath, Norbert. "Natur, zweite (II)." In *Historisches Wörterbuch der Philosophie*, vol. 6, 489–94.

———. *Zweite Natur: Konzepte einer Vermittlung von Natur und Kultur in Anthropologie und Ästhetik um 1800.* Münster: Waxmann, 1996.

Reyburn, Hugh. *Hegel's Ethical Theory.* Oxford: Clarendon, 1967.

Riedel, Manfred. "Framework and Meaning of 'Objective Spirit': A Conceptual Change in Political Philosophy." In his *Between Tradition & Revolution: The Hegelian Transformation of Political Philosophy*, translated by Walter Wright, 3–30. Cambridge: Cambridge University Press, 1984.

———. "Laws of Nature and Laws of Right: Problems in the Realization of Freedom." In his *Between Tradition & Revolution*, 57–75.

———, ed. *Materialien zu Hegels Rechtsphilosophie*, vol. 1. Frankfurt am Main: Suhrkamp, 1975.

———, ed. *Materialien zu Hegels Rechtsphilosophie*, vol. 2. Frankfurt am Main: Suhrkamp, 1975.

———. *Studien zu Hegels Rechtsphilosophie.* Frankfurt am Main: Suhrkamp, 1969.

Ritter, Joachim. *Hegel and the French Revolution: Essays on The Philosophy of Right*, translated by Richard Dien Winfield. Cambridge, Mass.: MIT Press, 1982.

———. *Metaphysik und Politik: Studien zu Aristoteles und Hegel.* Frankfurt am Main: Suhrkamp, 1969.

Rosenfield, Denis L. *Politique et liberté: Une étude sur la structure logique de la Philosophie du droit de Hegel.* Paris: Aubier, 1984.

Rosenzweig, Franz. *Hegel und der Staat*, edited by Frank Lachmann. 1920; Frankfurt am Main: Suhrkamp, 2010.

Schacht, Richard. "Hegel on Freedom." In *Hegel: A Collection of Critical Essays*, edited by Alasdair MacIntyre, 289–328. New York: Anchor Books, 1972.

Schild, Wolfgang. "Hegels Lehre vom Notrecht." In *Die Rechtsphilosophie des Deutschen Idealismus*, edited by Vittorio Hösle, 146–63. Hamburg: Meiner, 1989.

Schnädelbach, Herbert. "Zum Verhältnis von Logik und Gesellschaftstheorie bei Hegel." In *Aktualität und Folgen der Philosophie Hegels*, edited by Oskar Negt, 58–80. Frankfurt am Main: Suhrkamp, 1970.

Siep, Ludwig. "The 'Aufhebung' of Morality in Ethical Life." In *Hegel's Philosophy of Action*, edited by Lawrence S. Stepelevich and David Lamb, 137–55. Atlantic Highlands, N.J.: Humanities, 1983.

———, ed. *G. W. F. Hegel: Grundlinien der Philosophie des Rechts.* Berlin: Akademie Verlag, 1997.

Stepelevich, Lawrence S., and David Lamb, eds. *Hegel's Philosophy of Action.* Atlantic Highlands, N.J.: Humanities, 1983.

Stoeffer, F. E. *The Rise of Evangelical Pietism.* Leiden: Brill, 1965.

Taylor, Charles. *Hegel.* Cambridge: Cambridge University Press, 1975.

———. *Hegel and Modern Society.* Cambridge: Cambridge University Press, 1979.

———. "Hegel and the Philosophy of Action." In *Hegel's Philosophy of Action*, edited by Lawrence S. Stepelevich and David Lamb, 1–18. Atlantic Highlands, N.J.: Humanities, 1983.

Theis, Robert. "Volonté et liberté: Commentaire de l'Introduction à la Philosophie du Droit de Hegel." *Archiv für Rechts- und Sozialphilosophie* 65, no. 3 (1979): 369–86.

Troeltsch, Ernst. *The Social Teaching of the Christian Churches*, vol. 2. London: George Allen and Unwin, 1931.

Tugendhat, Ernst. *Self-Consciousness and Self-Determination*, translated by Paul Stern. Cambridge, Mass.: MIT Press, 1986.

Tunick, Mark. "Hegel's Nonfoundationalism: A Phenomenological Account of the Structure of the *Philosophy of Right*." *History of Philosophy Quarterly* 11 (1994): 317–37.

Vieweg, Klaus. *Das Denken der Freiheit: Hegels Grundlinien der Philosophie des Rechts.* Munich: Wilhelm Fink, 2011.

Walsh, W. H. *Hegelian Ethics.* London: Macmillan, 1969.

Weil, Eric. *Hegel and the State*, translated by Mark A. Cohen. Baltimore, Md.: Johns Hopkins University Press, 1998.

Weisser-Lohmann, Elisabeth. *Rechtsphilosophie als praktiche Philosophie: Hegels Grundlinien der Philosophie des Rechts und die Grundlegung der praktischen Philosophie.* Munich: Wilhelm Fink, 2011.

Winfield, Richard Dien. *Reason and Justice.* Albany: State University of New York Press, 1988.

Wood, Allen W. "Hegel's Critique of Morality." In *G. W. F. Hegel, Grundlinien der Philosophie des Rechts*, edited by Ludwig Siep, 147–66. Berlin: Akademie Verlag, 1997.

———. *Hegel's Ethical Thought.* Cambridge: Cambridge University Press, 1990.

Yeomans, Christopher. "'Acting On' Instead of 'Stepping Back': Hegel's Conception of the Relation between Motivations and the Free Will." In *Yo y Tiempo: La antropología filosófica de G.W.F. Hegel, vol. I: La sustancialidad y subjetividad humanas*, edited by I. Falgueras, J. A. García, and Juan J. Padial, *Contrastes*, Suplemento 15 (2010): 377–87.

———. *Freedom and Reflection: Hegel on the Logic of Agency.* Oxford: Oxford University Press, 2012.

Zabel, Benno. "The Institutional Turn in Hegel's Philosophy of Right: Towards a Conception of Freedom beyond Individualism and Collectivism." *Hegel Bulletin* 36, no. 1 (2015): 80–104.

Ziolkowski, Theodore. *German Romanticism and Its Institutions.* Princeton, N.J.: Princeton University Press, 1990.

INDEX